"Do you think that hum   David
Swanson makes perhaps as good   found.
Think of the death penalty. Once considered critical to our
security, the death penalty is now universally considered optional
and widely considered archaic, counter-productive, and shameful.
To an even greater extent, this has been the fate of slavery. Why
should war not suffer the same destiny?" —William Blum, author

"David Swanson does it again. Yet another tour de force against
war and for peace. This book is required reading for everyone in
the peace movement. As Swanson argues, we must abolish war
before war abolishes us. There will be no war criminals tribunal
after World War III. Swanson's book is a beacon of hope to a
frightened, paralyzed humanity." —Francis A. Boyle, professor

"*War No More* reminds us that war abolition can be as successful
as was slavery abolition—once we recognize that wars are made
by societies that tolerate war, and that wars can be avoided by a
cultural rejection of war. As long as Americans feel helpless about
their ability to have an impact on the U.S. government, wars will
continue, but Swanson's book and his life are antidotes to American
helplessness." —Bruce E. Levine, author

"I am always impressed and inspired by David's prolific energy
and I admire his unwavering opposition to *all war,* not just the
ones started or continued by Republicans. In *War No More*, David
once again lays out an impeccable case for abolishing war as a tool
of Empire." —Cindy Sheehan, author and peace activist

"Living in the most militarized culture on earth, we can get trapped into thinking that our choices are limited to going to war or doing nothing. In *War No More,* Swanson completely destroys this deadly myth. He convincingly, passionately shows there are many options available to our enormously creative minds once we decide war is not an option of last resort—it is no option at all. —Mike Ferner, former president, Veterans For Peace

"The ideas in this book have truly opened up a new way for me to think about war; or, to be more specific, ending it." —Sean McCord, playwright

"David Swanson writes like he talks; that is to say, in clear, sharp language that gets to the root of the issue, but in a very personal way...as if you are having a one-on-one conversation with him. As a natural follow-on to Swanson's previous books about war, *War Is A Lie,* and *When the World Outlawed War,* he brings us to the logical next step: ending war. Swanson shows us that abolishing war is not unfathomable, but that it will take more than just a change in mindset; it will take real action and real work—a *movement.* Count me in." —Leah Bolger, former president, Veterans For Peace

"Long ago, abolitionists caused huge discomfort. They still do. The work of David Swanson is in the vital spirit of William Lloyd Garrison, who had a clear answer when a friend urged him to keep more cool because he seemed on fire. 'I have need to be all on fire,' Garrison replied, 'for there are mountains of ice around me to melt.' Swanson's new book *War No More* generates an abundance of heat *and* light. It will serve as a powerful blowtorch for efforts to abolish war." —Norman Solomon, author

War No More
The Case for Abolition
by David Swanson

With a Foreword by Kathy Kelly

Charlottesville, VA
First edition—2013

Also by David Swanson
TUBE WORLD (2012)
THE MILITARY INDUSTRIAL COMPLEX AT 50 (2011)
WHEN THE WORLD OUTLAWED WAR (2011)
WAR IS A LIE (2010)
DAYBREAK: UNDOING THE IMPERIAL PRESIDENCY
AND FORMING A MORE PERFECT UNION (2009)
THE 35 ARTICLES OF IMPEACHMENT (Introduction, 2008)

davidswanson.org

•   •   •

Swanson, David, 1969 Dec. 1-

War No More: The Case for Abolition

Book design by David Swanson
Photo by Scott Strazzante, *Chicago Tribune*

Printed in the USA

First Edition / September 2013

ISBN: 978-0-9830830-5-4

CONTENTS

We do not care-
That much is clear.
Not enough
Of us care
Anywhere.
We are not wise-
For that reason,
Mankind dies.
To think
Is much against
The will.
Better-
And easier-
To kill.

—Langston Hughes

FOREWORD

I lived in Iraq during the 2003 Shock and Awe bombing. On April 1st, about two weeks into the aerial bombardment, a medical doctor who was one of my fellow peace team members urged me to go with her to the Al Kindi Hospital in Baghdad, where she knew she could be of some help. With no medical training, I tried to be unobtrusive, as families raced into the hospital carrying wounded loved ones. At one point, a woman sitting next to me began to weep uncontrollably. "How I tell him?" she asked, in broken English. "What I say?" She was Jamela Abbas, the aunt of a young man, named Ali. Early in the morning on March 31st, U.S. war planes had fired on her family home, while she alone of all her family was outside. Jamela wept as she searched for words to tell Ali that surgeons had amputated both of his badly damaged arms, close to his shoulders. What's more, she would have to tell him that she was now his sole surviving relative.

I soon heard how that conversation had gone. It was reported to me that when Ali, aged 12, learned that he had lost both of his arms, he responded by asking "Will I always be this way?"

Returning to the Al Fanar hotel, I hid in my room. Furious tears flowed. I remember pounding my pillow and asking "Will we always be this way?"

David Swanson reminds me to look to humanity's incredible achievements in resisting war, in choosing the alternatives which we have yet to show our full power to realize.

A hundred years ago, Eugene Debs campaigned tirelessly in the U.S. to build a better society, where justice and equality would prevail and ordinary people would no longer be sent to fight wars on behalf of tyrannical elites. From 1900 to 1920 Debs ran for president in each of five elections. He waged his 1920 campaign from inside the Atlanta prison to which he'd been sentenced for sedition for having spoken vigorously against U.S. entry into World War I. Insisting that wars throughout history have always been fought for purposes of conquest and plunder, Debs had distinguished between the master class that declares wars and the subjugated who fight the battles. "The master class has had all to gain and nothing to lose," said Debs in the speech for which he was imprisoned, "while the subject class has had nothing to gain and all to lose—especially their lives."

Debs hoped to create a mindset throughout the American electorate that withstood propaganda and rejected war. It was no easy process. As a labor historian writes, "With no radio and television spots, and with little sympathetic coverage of progressive, third party causes, there was no alternative but to travel incessantly, one city or whistle-stop at a time, in searing heat or numbing cold, before crowds large or small, in whatever hall, park or train station where a crowd could be assembled."

He didn't prevent U.S. entry into World War I, but Swanson tells us in his 2011 book, *When the World Outlawed War,* there came a point in U.S. history, in 1928, when wealthy elites decided that it was in their enlightened self-interest to negotiate the Kellogg-Briand Pact, intended to avert future wars, and to prevent future

U.S. governments from seeking war. Swanson encourages us to study and build on moments in history when war was rejected, and to refuse to tell ourselves that warfare is inevitable.

Surely we must join Swanson in acknowledging the enormous challenges we face in campaigning to avoid war, or to abolish it. He writes: "In addition to being immersed in a false world view of war's inevitability, people in the United States are up against corrupt elections, complicit media, shoddy education, slick propaganda, insidious entertainment, and a gargantuan permanent war machine falsely presented as a necessary economic program that cannot be dismantled." Swanson refuses to be deterred by large challenges. An ethical life is an extraordinary challenge, and encompasses lesser challenges, such as democratizing our societies. Part of the challenge is to honestly acknowledge its difficulty: to clear-sightedly witness the forces that make war more likely in our time and place, but Swanson refuses to categorize these forces as insurmountable obstacles.

A few years ago, I heard once more about Jamela Abbas' nephew, Ali. Now he was 16 years old, living in London where a BBC reporter had interviewed him. Ali had become an accomplished artist, using his toes to hold a paint brush. He had also learned to feed himself using his feet. "Ali," asked the interviewer, "what would you like to be when you grow up?" In perfect English, Ali had answered, "I'm not sure. But I would like to work for peace." David Swanson reminds us that we will not always be this way. We will transcend in ways that we cannot yet properly imagine, through the determination to rise above our incapacities and achieve our purposes on earth. Obviously Ali's story is not a feel-good story. Humanity has lost so much to war and what so often seems its incapacity for peace is like the most grievous of disfigurements. We don't know the ways we will discover in which to work to rise above these disfigurements. We learn from the past, we keep our eyes on our goal, we fully grieve our losses, and we expect to be surprised by the fruits of diligent labor and a passion to keep humanity alive, and to help it create again.

If David is right, if humanity survives, war itself will go the route of death-duels and infanticide, child labor and institutionalized slavery. Perhaps someday, beyond being made illegal, it will even be eliminated. Our other struggles for justice, against the slow grinding war of rich against poor, against the human sacrifice of capital punishment, against the tyranny that the fear of war so emboldens, feed into this one. Our organized movements working for these and countless other causes often are themselves models of peace, of coordination, a dissolution of isolation and of conflict in creative fellowship, the end of war made, in patches, already visible.

In Chicago, where I live, an annual summer extravaganza has been held on the lakefront for as long as I can remember. Called "The Air and Water Show," it grew in the past decade into a huge display of military force and a significant recruiting event. Prior to the big show, the Air Force would practice military maneuvers and we'd hear sonic booms throughout a week of preparation. The event would attract millions of people, and amid a picnic atmosphere the U.S. military potential to destroy and maim other people was presented as a set of heroic, triumphant adventures.

In the summer of 2013, word reached me in Afghanistan that the air and water show had occurred but that the U.S. military was a "no show."

My friend Sean had staked out a park entrance for the previous few yearly events in a solo protest, cheerily encouraging attendees to "enjoy the show" all the more for its incredible cost to them in tax dollars, in lives and global stability and political freedom lost to imperial militarization. Eager to acknowledge the human impulse to marvel at the impressive spectacle and technical achievement on display, he would insist of the planes, and in as friendly a tone as possible, "They look a lot cooler when they're not bombing you!" This year he was expecting smaller crowds, having heard (although apparently too busy assembling his several thousand fliers to closely research this year's particular event) that several military acts had cancelled. "Two hundred flyers later, I found out that this was because THE MILITARY HAD BACKED OUT!" he wrote me on the day itself: "They weren't there _at all_ save for some desultory Air Force tents that I did find when I biked through looking for recruitment stations. I suddenly understood why I hadn't heard any sonic booms leading up to the weekend." (I had always complained to Sean of the yearly agony of listening to those planes rehearse for the show) "Too pleased to be mortified by my own idiocy, I put away my fliers and biked happily through the event. It was a lovely morning, and the skies of Chicago had been healed!"

Our incapacities are never the whole story; our victories come in small cumulative ways that surprise us. A movement of millions arises to protest a war, whose onset is delayed, its impact lessened, by how many months or years, by how many lives never lost, by how many limbs never torn from the bodies of children? How completely are the cruel imaginations of the war-makers distracted by having to defend their current lethal plans, how many new outrages, thanks to our resistance, will they never so much as conceive? By how many factors as the years proceed will our demonstrations against war continue, with setbacks, to grow? How acutely will the humanity of our neighbors be aroused, to what level will their awareness be raised, how much more tightly knit in community will they learn to be in our shared efforts to challenge and resist war? Of course we can't know.

What we know is that we won't always be this way. War may exterminate us utterly, and if unchecked, unchallenged, it shows every potential for doing so. But David Swanson's *War No More* imagines a time where the Ali Abbases of the world exhibit their tremendous courage in a world that has abolished warfare, where no-one has to relive their tragedies at the hands of rampaging nations, where we celebrate the demise of war. Beyond this it envisions a time when humanity has found the true purpose, meaning, and community of its calling to end warfare together, to live the challenge that is replacing war with peace, discovering lives of resistance, and of truly human activity. Rather than glorify armed soldiers as heroes, let us appreciate a child rendered armless by a U.S. bomb who must know that few incapacities are an excuse for inaction, that what is or isn't possible changes, and who, despite all we've done to him, still resolutely intends to work for peace.

—Kathy Kelly

INTRODUCTION

As I write this, in September 2013, something extraordinary has just happened. Public pressure has led the British Parliament to refuse a prime minister's demand for war for the first time since the surrender at Yorktown, and the U.S. Congress has followed suit by making clear to the U.S. president that his proposed authorization for war on Syria would not pass through either the Senate or the House.

Now, this may all fall apart in a week or a month or a year or a decade. The forces pressing for a war on Syria have not gone away. The civil war and the humanitarian crisis in Syria are not over. The partisan makeup of the Parliament and the Congress played a role in their actions (although the leaders of both major parties in Congress favored attacking Syria). Foreign nations' intervention played a role. But the decisive force driving governments around the world and U.S. government (and military) insiders to resist this war was public opinion. We heard the stories of children suffering and dying in Syria, but we rejected the idea that killing more Syrians with U.S. weapons would make Syria better off.

Those of us who believe that we should always have the right to reject our government's arguments for war should feel empowered. Now that it's been done, we cannot be told it's impossible to do it again ... and again, and again.

In the space of a day, discussions in Washington, D.C., shifted from the supposed necessity of war to the clear desirability of avoiding war. If that can happen once, even if only momentarily, why can it not happen every time? Why cannot our government's eagerness for war be permanently done away with? U.S. Secretary of State John Kerry, who led the unsuccessful marketing campaign for an attack on Syria, had famously asked, many years earlier, during what the Vietnamese call the American War, "How do you ask a man to be the last man to die for a mistake?" We have it within our power to make war a thing of the past and to leave Secretary Kerry the last man to have tried to sell us a dead idea.

(An argument will be made that the threat of war aided diplomatic efforts to disarm the Syrian government. It should not be forgotten that when Kerry suggested that Syria could avoid a war by handing over its chemical weapons, everyone knew he didn't mean it. In fact, when Russia called his bluff and Syria immediately agreed, Kerry's staff put out this statement: "Secretary Kerry was making a rhetorical argument about the impossibility and unlikelihood of Assad turning over chemical weapons he has denied he used. His point was that this brutal dictator with a history of playing fast and loose with the facts cannot be trusted to turn over chemical weapons, otherwise he would have done so long ago. That's why the world faces this moment." In other words: stop getting in the way of our war! By the next day, however, with Congress rejecting war, Kerry was claiming to have meant his remark quite seriously and to believe the process had a good chance of succeeding.)

In this book I make the case outlined in the four section titles: War can be ended; War should be ended; War is not going to end on its own; We have to end war.

Others have made the case that war can be ended, but they have tended to look for the source of war in poor nations, overlooking the nation that builds, sells, buys, stockpiles, and uses the most weapons, engages in the most conflicts, stations the most troops in the most countries, and carries out the most deadly and destructive wars. By these and other measures, the United States government is the world's leading war-maker, and—in the words of Martin Luther King, Jr.—the greatest purveyor of violence in the world. Ending U.S. war-making wouldn't eliminate all war from the world, but ending war-making only by poor countries wouldn't come close.

This should not come as a shock or an offense to most people in the United States, some 80 percent of whom consistently tell pollsters that our government is broken. It's been over half a century since President Dwight Eisenhower warned that a military industrial complex would corrupt the United States. Military spending is roughly half of the U.S. government's discretionary spending every year, dwarfing any other expense. The United States is closely tied with the European Union as the wealthiest place on earth. Surely that money must be going somewhere. Surely a broken government is bound to be at least a little broken in the primary thing it does—in this case, the making of war.

By "war" I mean roughly: the use of a nation's military abroad. The use of a military at home to establish a police state or attack a sub-population is related to war and sometimes hard to distinguish from war, but usually distinct (the exceptions being called civil wars). The use of military-like tactics by a non-nation group or individual may sometimes be morally or visually indistinguishable from war, but it differs from war in terms of responsibility and appropriate response. The use of a nation's military abroad for purely non-war purposes, such as humanitarian relief, is not what I mean by war, and also not easy to find actual examples of. By the term "military," I mean to include uniformed and non-uniformed, official troops and contractors, acknowledged and clandestine—anyone (or any robot) engaged in military activity for a government.

I intend this book for people everywhere, but especially in the United States and the West. Most people in the United States do not believe that war can be ended. And I suspect that most are aware of the significant role the United States plays in war-making, because most also believe that war *should* not be ended. Few actually view war as desirable—once a widespread belief, but one heard less and less since about the time of World War I. Rather, people tend to believe that war is necessary to protect them or to prevent something worse than war.

So, in Part II, I make the case that war endangers, rather than protecting us, and that there isn't something worse than war that war can be used to prevent. I argue that war is not justified by evil forces it opposes or by false claims to humanitarian purposes. War is not benefitting us at home or the people in the nations where our wars are fought, out of sight and sometimes out of mind. War kills huge numbers of innocent people, ruins nations, devastates the natural environment, drains the economy, breeds hostility, and strips away civil liberties at home no matter how many times we say "freedom."

This case is not so much philosophical as factual. The most significant cause of war, I believe and argue in the book, is bad information about past wars. A majority in the United States believes Iraq benefitted from the 2003-2011 war that destroyed Iraq. If I believed that, I'd favor launching another one right away. A majority in Iraq believes the war left them even worse off than they were before it. (See, for example, the Zogby poll of December 20, 2011.) Extensive evidence, discussed below, as well as basic common sense, suggests that Iraqis, like anyone else, actually know best what their own situation is. Therefore, I want to prevent a repeat.

I wish I could have written a theoretical case against war, without mentioning any wars. But, everyone would have agreed with it and then made exceptions, like the school board member where I live who said he wanted to support a celebration of peace as long as everyone was clear he wasn't opposing any wars. As it is, I had to include actual wars, and facts about them. Where I've suspected someone will object to a piece of information, I've included a source for it right in the text. I discuss in this book the wars launched when George W. Bush was president and the wars launched or escalated since Barack Obama became president, as well as some of the most cherished "good wars" in U.S. culture, such as World War II and the U.S. Civil War. I also recommend reading this book in combination with a previous book of mine called *War Is A Lie*.

I don't recommend taking my word for anything. I encourage independent research. And a few other points may help with keeping an open-mind while reading this book: There's no partisan agenda here. The Democrats and Republicans are partners in war, and I have no loyalty to either of them. There's no national agenda here. I'm not interested in defending or attacking the U.S. government, or any other government. I'm interested in the facts about war and peace and what we should do about them. There's no political agenda here on the spectrum from libertarian to socialist. I certainly place myself on the socialist side of that spectrum, but on the question of war it's not particularly relevant. I think Switzerland has had a pretty good foreign policy. I admire Costa Rica's elimination of its military. Sure, I think useful and essential things should be done with the money that's now dumped into war and war preparations, but I'd favor ending war if the money were never collected or even if it were collected and burned.

Disturbing as it is to run into countless people who believe war can't and/or shouldn't be ended (including quite a few who say it can't be ended but should be ended, presumably meaning that they wish it could be ended but are sure it can't be), I've begun running into people who tell me—even more disturbingly—that war is in the process of ending, so there's nothing to worry about and nothing to be done. The arguments that have set people on this path distort and minimize death counts in recent wars, define large portions of wars as civil wars (and thus not wars), measure casualties in isolated wars against the entire population of the globe, and conflate downward trends in other types of violence with trends in war-making. Part III, therefore, makes the case that war is not, in fact, going away.

Part IV addresses how we should go about causing war to go away. Largely, I believe that we need to take steps to improve our production, distribution, and consumption of information, including by adjusting our worldviews to make ourselves more open to learning and understanding unpleasant facts about the world—and acting on them. More difficult tasks than the abolition of war have been accomplished before. The first step has usually been recognizing that we have a problem.

I. WAR CAN BE ENDED

Slavery Was Abolished

In the late eighteenth century the majority of people alive on earth were held in slavery or serfdom (three-quarters of the earth's population, in fact, according to the *Encyclopedia of Human Rights* from Oxford University Press). The idea of abolishing something so pervasive and long-lasting as slavery was widely considered ridiculous. Slavery had always been with us and always would be. One couldn't wish it away with naive sentiments or ignore the mandates of our human nature, unpleasant though they might be. Religion and science and history and economics all purported to prove slavery's permanence, acceptability, and even desirability. Slavery's existence in the Christian Bible justified it in the eyes of many. In *Ephesians 6:5* St. Paul instructed slaves to obey their earthly masters as they obeyed Christ.

Slavery's prevalence also allowed the argument that if one country didn't do it another country would: "Some gentlemen may, indeed, object to the slave trade as inhuman and evil," said a member of the British Parliament on May 23, 1777, "but let us consider that, if our colonies are to be cultivated, which can only be done by African negroes, it is surely better to supply ourselves with those labourers in British ships, than buy them from French, Dutch or Danish traders." On April 18, 1791, Banastre Tarleton declared in Parliament—and, no doubt, some even believed him—that "the Africans themselves have no objection to the trade."

By the end of the nineteenth century, slavery was outlawed nearly everywhere and rapidly on the decline. In part, this was because a handful of activists in England in the 1780s began a movement advocating for abolition, a story well told in Adam Hochschild's *Bury the Chains*. This was a movement that made ending the slave trade and slavery a moral cause, a cause to be sacrificed for on behalf of distant, unknown people very different from oneself. It was a movement of public pressure. It did not use violence and it did not use voting. Most people had no right to vote. Instead it used so-called naive sentiments and the active ignoring of the supposed mandates of our supposed human nature. It changed the culture, which is, of course, what regularly inflates and tries to preserve itself by calling itself "human nature."

Other factors contributed to the demise of slavery, including the resistance of the people enslaved. But such resistance was not new in the world. Widespread condemnation of slavery—including by former slaves—and a commitment not to allow its return: that was new and decisive.

Those ideas spread by forms of communication we now consider primitive. There is some evidence that in this age of instant global communication we can spread worthy ideas much more quickly.

So, is slavery gone? Yes and no. While owning another human being is banned and in disrepute around the world, forms of bondage still exist in certain places. There is not a hereditary caste of people enslaved for life, transported and bred and whipped openly by their owners, what might be called "traditional slavery." Sadly, however, debt slavery and sex slavery hide in various countries. There are pockets of slavery of various sorts in the United States. There is prison labor, with the laborers disproportionately being descendants of former slaves. There are more African-Americans behind bars or under supervision by the criminal justice system in the United States today than there were African-Americans enslaved in the United States in 1850.

But these modern evils don't convince anybody that slavery, in any form, is a permanent fixture in our world, and they shouldn't. Most African-Americans are not imprisoned. Most workers in the world are not enslaved in any type of slavery. In 1780, if you had proposed making slavery the exception to the rule, a scandal to be carried out in secret, hidden away and disguised where it still existed in any form, you would have been considered as naive and ignorant as someone proposing the complete elimination of slavery. If you were to propose bringing back slavery in a major way today, most people would denounce the idea as backward and barbaric.

All forms of slavery may not have been completely eliminated, and may never be. But they could be. Or, on the other hand, traditional slavery could be returned to popular acceptance and restored to prominence in a generation or two. Look at the rapid revival in acceptance of the use of torture in the early twenty-first century for an example of how a practice that some societies had begun to leave behind has been significantly restored. In this moment, however, it is clear to most people that slavery is a choice and that its abolition is an option—that, in fact, its abolition always was an option, even if a difficult one.

A Good Civil War?

In the United States some may have a tendency to doubt the abolition of slavery as a model for the abolition of war because war was used to end slavery. But did it have to be used? Would it have to be used today? Slavery was ended without war, through compensated emancipation, in the British colonies, Denmark, France, the Netherlands, and most of South America and the Caribbean. That model worked also in Washington, D.C. Slave owning states in the United States rejected it, most of them choosing secession instead. That's the way history went, and many people would have had to think very differently for it to have gone otherwise. But the cost of freeing the slaves by buying them would have been far less than the North spent on the war, not counting what the South spent, not counting the deaths and injuries, mutilations, trauma, destruction, and decades of bitterness to come, while slavery long remained nearly real in all but name. (See *Costs of Major U.S. Wars,* by the Congressional Research Service, June 29, 2010.)

On June 20, 2013, the *Atlantic* published an article called "No, Lincoln Could Not Have 'Bought the Slaves.'" Why not? Well, the slave owners didn't want to sell. That's perfectly true. They didn't, not at all. But the *Atlantic* focuses on another argument, namely that it would have just been too expensive, costing as much as $3 billion (in 1860s money). Yet, if you read closely—it's easy to miss it—the author admits that the war cost over twice that much. The cost of freeing people was simply unaffordable. Yet the cost—over twice as much—of killing people, goes by almost unnoticed. As with well-fed people's appetites for desserts, there seems to be a completely separate compartment for war spending, a compartment kept far away from criticism or even questioning.

The point is not so much that our ancestors could have made a different choice (they were nowhere near doing so), but that their choice looks foolish from our point of view. If tomorrow we were to wake up and discover everyone appropriately outraged over the horror of mass incarceration, would it help to find some large fields in which to kill each other off in large numbers? What would that have to do with abolishing prisons? And what did the Civil War have to do with abolishing slavery? If—radically contrary to actual history—U.S. slave owners had opted to end slavery without war, it's hard to imagine that as a bad decision.

Let me try to really, really emphasize this point: what I am describing DID NOT happen and was not about to happen, was nowhere remotely close to happening; but its happening would have been a good thing. Had slave owners and politicians radically altered their thinking and chosen to end slavery without a war, they would have ended it with less suffering, and probably ended it more completely. In any case, to imagine slavery ending without war, we need only look at the actual history of various other countries. And to imagine big changes being made in our society today (whether it's closing prisons, creating solar arrays, rewriting the Constitution, facilitating sustainable agriculture, publicly financing elections, developing democratic media outlets, or anything else—you may not like any of these ideas, but I'm sure you can think of a major change that you *would* like) we don't tend to include as Step 1 "Find large fields in which to make our children kill each other in huge numbers." Instead, we skip right by that to Step 2 "Do the thing that needs doing." And so we should.

Existence Precedes Essence

To any philosopher sharing Jean Paul Sartre's outlook on the world there is no need to demonstrate the virtual abolition of slavery in order to be convinced that slavery is optional. We're human beings, and for Sartre that means we're free. Even when enslaved, we're free. We can choose not to speak, not to eat, not to drink, not to have sex. As I was writing this, large numbers of prisoners were engaged in a hunger strike in California and in Guantanamo Bay and in Palestine (and they were in touch with each other). Everything is optional, always has been, always will be. If we can choose not to eat, we can certainly choose not to engage in the extensive effort, requiring the collaboration of many people, to establish or maintain the institution of slavery. From this viewpoint it is simply obvious that we can choose not to enslave people. We can choose universal love or cannibalism or whatever we see fit. Parents tell their children, "You can be anything you choose to be," and the same must also be true of the assembled collection of everyone's children.

I think the above viewpoint, naive as it may sound, is essentially right. It doesn't mean that future events are not physically determined by past ones. It means that, from the perspective of a non-omniscient human being, choices are available. This doesn't mean you can choose to have physical abilities or talents you don't have. It doesn't mean you can choose how the rest of the world behaves. You can't choose to have a billion dollars or win a gold medal or get elected president. But you can choose to be the sort of person who wouldn't own a billion dollars while others starved, or the sort of person who would do just that and focus on owning two billion dollars. You can choose your own behavior. You can give winning a gold medal or getting rich or getting elected your best effort or a half-hearted effort or no effort at all. You can be the sort of person who obeys illegal or immoral orders, or the sort of person who defies them. You can be the sort of person who tolerates or encourages something like slavery or the sort of person who struggles to abolish it even as many others support it. And because we can *each* choose to abolish it, I will argue, we can *collectively* choose to abolish it.

There are a number of ways in which someone might disagree with this. Perhaps, they might suggest, some powerful force prevents us all from collectively choosing what we might each choose as an individual in a moment of calm clarity. This force could simply be a sort of social irrationality or the inevitable influence of sycophants on the powerful. Or it could be the pressure of economic competition or population density or resource shortages. Or perhaps some segment of our population is sick or damaged in a way that compels them to create the institution of slavery. These individuals could impose the institution of slavery on the rest of the world. Perhaps the slavery-inclined portion of the population includes all males, and women are unable to overcome the masculine drive toward slavery. Maybe the corruption of power, combined with the self-selection of those inclined to seek power makes destructive public policies inevitable. Maybe the influence of profiteers and the skill of propagandists render us helpless to resist. Or perhaps a large portion of the globe could be organized to end slavery, but some other society would always bring slavery back like a contagious disease, and ending it simultaneously everywhere would just not be feasible. Maybe capitalism inevitably produces slavery, and capitalism is itself inevitable. Maybe human destructiveness targeted toward the natural environment necessitates slavery. Maybe racism or nationalism or religion or xenophobia or patriotism or exceptionalism or fear or greed or a general lack of empathy is itself inevitable and guarantees slavery no matter how hard we try to think and act our way out of it.

These sorts of claims for inevitability sound less persuasive when addressed to an institution that has already been largely eliminated, like slavery. I'll address them below with regard to the institution of war. Certain of these theories—population density, resource scarcity, etc.—are more popular among academics who look to non-Western nations as the primary source for war making. Other theories, such as the influence of what President Dwight Eisenhower called the military industrial complex, are more popular among discouraged peace activists in the United States. It's not unusual, however, to hear supporters of U.S. wars cite the supposed need to fight for resources and "lifestyle" as a justification for wars that have been presented on television as having entirely different motivations. I will hope to make clear that claims for the inevitability of slavery or war have no basis in fact, whichever institution they are applied to. The plausibility of this argument will be helped if we first consider just how many venerable institutions we have already left behind.

Blood Feuds and Duels

Nobody in the United States is proposing to bring back blood feuds, revenge killings of members of one family by members of a different family. Such retaliatory slaughters were once a common and accepted practice in Europe and are still very much around in some parts of the world. The infamous Hatfields and McCoys have not drawn each other's blood for over a century. In 2003, these two U.S. families finally signed a truce. Blood feuds in the United States had long since been effectively stigmatized and rejected by a society that believed it could do better and has done better.

Sadly, one of the McCoys involved in signing the truce made less than ideal comments, while the United States waged war in Iraq. According to the *Orlando Sentinel,* "Reo Hatfield of Waynesboro, Va., came up with the idea as a proclamation of peace. The broader message it sends to the world, he said, is that when national security is at risk, Americans put their differences aside and stand united." According to CBS News, "Reo said after Sept. 11 he wanted to make an official statement of peace between the two families to show that if the most deep-seeded [*sic*] family feud can be mended, so can the nation unite to protect its freedom." The nation. Not the world. "Protect freedom" in June 2003 was code for "fight war," regardless of whether the war, like most wars, reduced our freedoms.

Have we remade family blood feuds as national blood feuds? Have we stopped killing the neighbors over stolen pigs or inherited grievances because a mysterious force that compels us to kill has been redirected into killing foreigners through war? Would Kentucky go to war with West Virginia, and Indiana with Illinois, if they couldn't go to war with Afghanistan instead? Is Europe finally at peace with itself only because it's constantly helping the United States attack places like Afghanistan, Iraq, and Libya? Didn't President George W. Bush justify a war on Iraq in some part by alleging that Iraq's president had tried to kill Bush's father? Doesn't the United States treat Cuba as though the Cold War never ended largely because of sheer inertia? After he killed a U.S. citizen named Anwar al-Awlaki, didn't President Barack Obama send another missile two weeks later that killed Awlaki's 16-year-old son, against whom no accusations of wrong doing have ever been made? If—bizarre coincidence though it would be—the younger Awlaki was targeted without having been identified, or if he and the other young people with him were killed through pure recklessness, doesn't the resemblance to blood feuds still hold?

Certainly, but a resemblance is not an equivalence. Blood feuds, as they were, are gone from U.S. culture and many other cultures around the world. Blood feuds were, at one point, considered normal, natural, admirable, and permanent. They were required by tradition and honor, by family and morality. But, in the United States and many other places, they are gone. Their vestiges remain. Blood feuds appear again in milder form, without the blood, sometimes with lawyers substituted for shotguns. Traces of blood feuds attach themselves to current practices, such as war, or gang violence, or criminal prosecutions and sentencings. But blood feuds are in no way central to existing wars, they don't cause wars, the wars don't follow their logic. Blood feuds have not been transformed into war or anything else. They've been abolished. War existed before and after the elimination of blood feuds, and had more similarities to blood feuds prior to their elimination than after. The governments that fight wars have internally imposed a ban on violence, but the ban has only succeeded where people have accepted its authority, where people have agreed that blood feuds must be left behind us. There are parts of the world where people have not accepted that.

Dueling

Revival of dueling seems even less likely than a return to slavery or blood feuds. Duels were once commonplace in Europe and the United States. Militaries, including the U.S. Navy, used to lose more officers to dueling among themselves than to combat with a foreign enemy. Dueling was banned, stigmatized, mocked, and rejected during the nineteenth century as a barbaric practice. People collectively decided it could be left behind, and it was.

No one proposed to eliminate aggressive or unjust dueling while keeping defensive or humanitarian dueling in place. The same can be said of blood feuds and slavery. These practices were rejected as a whole, not modified or civilized. We don't have Geneva Conventions to regulate proper slavery or civilized blood feuds. Slavery wasn't maintained as an acceptable practice for some people. Blood feuds were not tolerated for certain special families who needed to be prepared to fend off the irrational or evil families who couldn't be reasoned with. Dueling has not remained legal and acceptable for particular personages. The United Nations doesn't authorize duels the way it authorizes wars. Dueling, in the countries that formerly engaged in it, is understood to be a destructive, backward, primitive, and ignorant way for individuals to try to settle their disputes. Whatever insult someone may hurl at you is almost certain to be milder—as we view things today— than an accusation of being so stupid and vicious as to participate in duels. Therefore dueling is no longer a means to protect one's reputation from insult.

Does the occasional duel still happen? Probably, but so does the occasional (or not so occasional) murder, rape, and theft. No one is proposing to legalize those, and nobody is proposing to bring back dueling. We generally try to teach our children to settle their disputes with words, not fists or weapons. When we can't work things out, we ask friends or a supervisor or the police or a court or some other authority to arbitrate or impose a ruling. We haven't eliminated disputes between individuals, but we have learned that we're all better off settling them nonviolently. At some level most of us understand that even the person who might have been victorious in a duel but who loses in a court ruling is still better off. That person does not have to live in as violent a world, does not have to suffer from his "victory," does not have to witness the suffering of his adversary's loved ones, does not have to seek satisfaction or "closure" in vain through the elusive sensation of vengeance, does not have to fear any loved one's death or injury in a duel, and does not have to stay prepared for his own next duel to come.

International Duels:
Spain, Afghanistan, Iraq

What if war is as bad a way to settle international disputes as dueling is to settle interpersonal disputes? The similarities are perhaps sharper than we care to imagine. Duels were contests between pairs of men who had decided that their disagreements could not be settled by speaking. Of course, we know better. They could have resolved matters by speaking, but chose not to. No one was obliged to fight a duel because someone he was arguing with was irrational. Anyone who chose to fight a duel wanted to fight a duel, and was himself—therefore—impossible for the other person to talk to.

Wars are contests between nations (even when described as being fought against something like "terror")—nations unable to settle their disagreements by speaking. We ought to know better. Nations could resolve their disputes by speaking, but choose not to. No nation is obliged to fight a war because another nation is irrational. Any nation that chooses to fight a war wanted to fight a war, and was itself—therefore—impossible for the other nation to talk to. This is the pattern we see in many U.S. wars.

The good side (our own side, of course) in a war, we like to believe, has been compelled into it because the other side understands only violence. You just can't talk to Iranians, for example. It would be nice if you could, but this is the real world, and in the real world certain nations are run by mythical monsters incapable of rational thought!

Let's assume for the sake of argument that governments make war because the other side won't be reasonable and talk to them. Many of us don't actually believe this is true. We see war-making as driven by irrational desires and greed, war justifications as packages of lies. I actually wrote a book called *War Is A Lie* surveying the most common types of lies about wars. But, for the sake of a comparison with dueling, let's look at the case for war as a last resort when talking fails, and see how it holds up. And let's look at cases involving the United States, as they are most familiar to many of us and somewhat familiar to many others, and as the United States (as I'll discuss below) is the world's leading maker of war.

Spain

The theory that war is a last resort used against those who cannot be reasoned with does not hold up well. The Spanish-American War (1898), for example, doesn't quite fit. Spain was willing to submit to the judgment of any neutral arbiter, after the United States accused the Spanish of blowing up a ship called the *U.S.S. Maine,* but the United States was insistent upon going to war despite having no evidence to support its accusations against Spain, accusations that served as the war's justification. To make sense of our theory of war we have to place Spain in the role of rational actor and the United States in the role of lunatic. *That* can't be right.

Seriously: it can't be right. The United States was not run by and was not inhabited by lunatics. Sometimes it can be hard to see in what way lunatics could do worse than our elected officials are doing, but the fact remains that Spain was not dealing with subhuman monsters, merely with Americans. And the United States was not dealing with subhuman monsters, merely with Spaniards. The matter could have been settled around a table, and one side even made that proposal. The fact is that the United States wanted war, and there was nothing the Spanish could say to prevent it. The United States chose war, just as a dueler chose to duel.

Afghanistan

Examples spring to mind from more recent history too, not just from centuries gone by. The United States, for three years prior to September 11, 2001, had been asking the Taliban to turn over Osama bin Laden. The Taliban had asked for evidence of his guilt of any crimes and a commitment to try him in a neutral third country without the death penalty. This continued right into October, 2001. (See, for example "Bush Rejects Taliban Offer to Hand Bin Laden Over" in *the Guardian,* October 14, 2001.) The Taliban's demands don't seem irrational or crazy. They seem like the demands of someone with whom negotiations might be continued. The Taliban also warned the United States that bin Laden was planning an attack on U.S. soil (this according to the BBC). Former Pakistani Foreign Secretary Niaz Naik told the BBC that senior U.S. officials told him at a U.N.-sponsored summit in Berlin in July 2001 that the United States would take action against the Taliban in mid-October. He said it was doubtful that surrendering bin Laden would change those plans. When the United States attacked Afghanistan on October 7, 2001, the Taliban asked again to negotiate handing over bin Laden to a third country to be tried. The United States rejected the offer and continued a war in Afghanistan for many years, not halting it when bin Laden was believed to have left that country, and not even halting it after announcing bin Laden's death. (See *Foreign Policy Journal,* September 20, 2010.) Perhaps there were other reasons to keep the war going for a dozen years, but clearly the reason to begin it was not that no other means of resolving the dispute were available. Clearly the United States wanted war.

Why would someone want war? As I argue in *War Is A Lie,* the United States wasn't so much seeking vengeance for Spain's supposed destruction of the *Maine* as grabbing an opportunity to conquer territories. Invading Afghanistan had little or nothing to do with bin Laden or a government that had helped bin Laden. Rather, U.S. motivations were related to fossil fuel pipelines, the positioning of weaponry, political posturing, geo-political posturing, maneuvering toward an invasion of Iraq (Tony Blair told Bush Afghanistan had to come first), patriotic cover for power grabs and unpopular policies at home, and profiteering from war and its expected spoils. The United States wanted war.

The United States has less than 5 percent of the world's population but uses one-third of the world's paper, a quarter of the world's oil, 23 percent of the coal, 27 percent of the aluminum, and 19 percent of the copper. (See *Scientific American,* September 14, 2012.) That state of affairs cannot be indefinitely continued through diplomacy. "The hidden hand of the market will never work without a hidden fist. McDonald's cannot flourish without McDonnell Douglas, the designer of the U.S. Air Force F-15. And the hidden fist that keeps the world safe for Silicon Valley's technologies to flourish is called the U.S. Army, Air Force, Navy and Marine Corps," says hidden hand enthusiast and *New York Times* columnist Thomas Friedman. But greed is not an argument for the other guy's irrationality or viciousness. It's just greed. We've all seen young children and even older people learn to be less greedy. There are also paths toward sustainable energies and local economies that lead away from wars of greed without leading to suffering or impoverishment. Most calculations of large-scale conversion to green energy don't take into account the transfer of enormous resources from the military. We'll discuss what ending war makes possible below. The point here is that war does not deserve to be considered more respectable than dueling.

Was war inevitable from the point of view of Afghans, who found the United States uninterested in negotiations? Certainly not. While violent resistance has failed to end the war for over a decade, it is possible that nonviolent resistance would have been more successful. We can benefit, as those in centuries past could not, from the history of nonviolent resistance in the Arab Spring, in Eastern Europe, in South Africa, in India, in Central America, in successful efforts by Filipinos and Puerto Ricans to close U.S. military bases, etc.

Lest this sound like I am just offering unwanted advice to Afghans while my government bombs them, I should point out that the same lesson can apply in my country as well. The U.S. public supports or tolerates the spending (through a variety of departments—consult the War Resisters League or the National

Priorities Project) of over $1 trillion every year on war preparations precisely because of the fear (fantastical though it may be) of an invasion of the United States by a foreign power. Should that happen, the foreign power involved would likely be destroyed by U.S. weapons. But, were we to dismantle those weapons, we would not—contrary to popular opinion—be left defenseless. We would be able to refuse our cooperation with the occupation. We could recruit fellow resisters from the invading nation and human shields from around the world. We could pursue justice through public opinion, courts, and sanctions targeted at the individuals responsible.

In reality, it is the United States and NATO that invade others. The war on and occupation of Afghanistan, if we step back from it just a little, appears as barbaric as a duel. Punishing a government willing (on certain reasonable conditions) to turn over an accused criminal, by spending well over a decade bombing and killing that nation's people (most of whom had never heard of the attacks of September 11, 2001, much less supported them, and most of whom hated the Taliban) doesn't appear to be a significantly more civilized action than shooting a neighbor because his great-uncle stole your grandfather's pig. In fact war kills a lot more people than blood feuds. Twelve years later, the U.S. government, as I write this, is trying to negotiate with the Taliban—a flawed process in that the people of Afghanistan are not well-represented by either party in the negotiations, but a process which could have better taken place 12 years earlier. If you can talk to them now, why couldn't you talk to them then, prior to the elaborate mass-duel? If a war on Syria can be avoided, why couldn't a war on Afghanistan?

Iraq

Then there's the case of Iraq in March 2003. The United Nations had refused to authorize an attack on Iraq, just as it had refused two years earlier with Afghanistan. Iraq was not threatening the United States. The United States possessed and was preparing to use against Iraq all sorts of internationally condemned weaponry: white phosphorous, new kinds of napalm, cluster bombs, depleted uranium. The U.S. plan was to attack infrastructure and densely populated areas with such fury that, contrary to all past experience, the people would be "shocked and awed"—another word would be *terrorized*—into submission. And the justification put forth for this was Iraq's supposed possession of chemical, biological, and nuclear weapons.

Unfortunately for these plans, a process of international inspections had rid Iraq of such weapons years before and confirmed their absence. Inspections were underway, re-confirming the complete absence of such weapons, when the United States announced that the war would begin and the inspectors must leave. The war was needed, the U.S. government claimed, to overthrow the government of Iraq—to remove Saddam Hussein from power. However, according to a transcript of a meeting in February 2003 between President George W. Bush and the Prime Minister of Spain, Bush said that Hussein had offered to leave Iraq, and to go into exile, if he could keep $1 billion. (See *El Pais,* September 26, 2007, or the *Washington Post* of the following day.) The *Washington Post* commented: "Although Bush's public position at the time of the meeting was that the door remained open for a diplomatic solution, hundreds of thousands of U.S. troops had already been deployed to Iraq's border, and the White House had made its impatience clear. 'Time is short,' Bush said in a news conference with [Spanish Prime Minister Jose Maria] Aznar the same day."

Perhaps a dictator being allowed to flee with $1 billion is not an ideal outcome. But the offer was not revealed to the U.S. public. We were told that diplomacy was impossible. Negotiation was impossible, we were told. (Thus, there was no opportunity to make a counter offer of a half a billion dollars, for example.) Inspections hadn't worked, they said. The weapons were there and could be used at any moment against us, they said. War, regretfully, tragically, sorrowfully was the last resort, they told us. President Bush and British Prime Minister Tony Blair spoke at the White House on January 31, 2003, claiming that war would be avoided if at all possible, just after a private meeting in which Bush had suggested flying U2 reconnaissance aircraft with fighter cover over Iraq, painted in U.N. colors, and hoping Iraq would fire on them, as that would supposedly have been grounds to start the war. (See *Lawless World* by Phillipe Sands, and see the extensive media coverage collected at WarIsACrime.org/WhiteHouseMemo.)

Rather than losing a billion dollars, the people of Iraq lost an estimated 1.4 million lives, saw 4.5 million people made refugees, their nation's infrastructure and education and health systems destroyed, civil liberties lost that had existed even under Saddam Hussein's brutal rule, environmental destruction almost beyond imagining, epidemics of disease and birth defects as horrific as the world has known. The nation of Iraq was destroyed. The cost to Iraq or to the United States in dollars was far more than a billion (the United States paid over $800 billion, not counting trillions of dollars in increased fuel costs, future interest payments, veterans' care, and lost opportunities). (See DavidSwanson.org/Iraq .) None of this was done because Iraq couldn't be reasoned with.

The U.S. government, at the top level, wasn't motivated by the fictional weapons at all. And it's not actually the place of the U.S. government to decide for Iraq whether its dictator flees. The U.S. government should have worked on ending its support for dictators in many other countries before interfering with Iraq in a new way. The option existed of ending the economic sanctions and bombings and beginning to make reparations. But if the United States' stated motivations had been its real ones, we could conclude that talking was an option that should have been chosen. Negotiating Iraq's withdrawal from Kuwait had been an option at the time of the First Gulf War as well. Choosing not to support and empower Hussein had been an option earlier still. There is always an alternative to backing violence. This is true even from the Iraqi point of view. Resistance to oppression can be nonviolent or violent.

Examine any war you like, and it turns out that if the aggressors had wanted to state their desires openly, they could have entered into negotiations rather than into battle. Instead, they wanted war—war for its own sake, or war for completely indefensible reasons that no other nation would willingly agree to.

War Is Optional

During the Cold War, the Soviet Union actually shot at and, in fact, shot down a U2 plane, the very act that President Bush hoped would launch a war on Iraq, but the United States and the Soviet Union talked the matter over instead of going to war. That option always exists—even when the threat of mutual annihilation is not present. It existed with the Bay of Pigs and Cuban Missile Crises. When warmongers in President John F. Kennedy's administration tried to trap him into a war, he chose instead to fire top officials and continue to talk to the Soviet Union, where a similar push for war was playing out and being resisted by Chairman Nikita Khrushchev. (Read James Douglass' *JFK and the Unspeakable.*) In recent years, proposals to attack Iran or Syria have been repeatedly rejected. Those attacks may come, but they are optional.

In March 2011, the African Union had a plan for peace in Libya but was prevented by NATO, through the creation of a "no fly" zone and the initiation of bombing, to travel to Libya to discuss it. In April, the African Union was able to discuss its plan with Libyan President Muammar al-Gaddafi, and he expressed his agreement. NATO, which had obtained a U.N. authorization to protect Libyans alleged to be in danger but no authorization to continue bombing the country or to overthrow the government, continued bombing the country and overthrowing the government. One may believe that was a good thing to do. "We came. We saw. He died!" said a triumphant U.S. Secretary of State Hillary Clinton, laughing joyfully after the death of Gaddafi. (Watch the video at WarIsACrime.org/Hillary.) Similarly, duelists believed shooting the other guy was a good thing to do. The point here is that it was not the only available option. As with dueling, wars could be replaced with dialogue and arbitration. The aggressor might not always get out of diplomacy what the insiders behind the war-making secretly and shamefully want, but would that be such a bad thing?

This is true with the long-threatened possible U.S. war on Iran. The Iranian government's attempts at negotiation have been rejected by the United States for the past decade. In 2003, Iran proposed negotiations with everything on the table, and the United States dismissed the offer. Iran has agreed to greater restrictions on its nuclear program than required by law. Iran has attempted to agree to U.S. demands, repeatedly agreeing to ship nuclear fuel out of the country. In 2010, Turkey and Brazil went to a great deal of trouble to get Iran to agree to just what the U.S. government said was needed, which resulted only in the U.S. government expressing its anger toward Turkey and Brazil.

If what the United States really wants is to dominate Iran and exploit its resources, Iran cannot be expected to compromise by accepting partial domination. That goal shouldn't be pursued by diplomacy or war. If what the United States really wants is for other nations to abandon nuclear energy, it may find it difficult to impose that policy on them, with or without the use of war. The most likely path to success would be neither war nor negotiations, but example and aid. The United States could begin dismantling its nuclear weapons and power plants. It could invest in green energy. The financial resources available for green energy, or anything else, if the war machine were dismantled are almost unfathomable. The

United States could offer green energy assistance to the world for a fraction of what it spends to offer military domination—not to mention lifting the sanctions that prevent Iran from acquiring parts for windmills.

Wars Against Individuals

Examining wars fought against individuals and small bands of alleged terrorists also shows that talking has been an available, albeit rejected, option. In fact, it's hard to find a case in which killing appears to have been the last resort. In May 2013 President Obama gave a speech in which he claimed that of all the people he'd killed with drone strikes only four had been U.S. citizens, and in one out of those four cases he had met certain criteria he'd created for himself prior to authorizing the killing. All publicly available information contradicts that claim, and in fact the U.S. government was trying to kill Anwar al-Awlaki before the incidents occurred in which President Obama later claimed Awlaki played a part that justified his killing. But Awlaki was never charged with a crime, never indicted, and his extradition never sought. On June 7, 2013, Yemeni tribal leader Saleh Bin Fareed told *Democracy Now* that Awlaki could have been turned over and put on trial, but "they never asked us." In numerous other cases it is evident that drone strike victims could have been arrested if that avenue had ever been attempted. (A memorable example was the November 2011 drone killing in Pakistan of 16-year-old Tariq Aziz, days after he'd attended an anti-drone meeting in the capital, where he might easily have been arrested—had he been charged with some crime.) Perhaps there are reasons for the preference of killing over capturing. But, then again, perhaps there were reasons why people preferred fighting duels to filing law suits.

The idea of enforcing laws against individuals by shooting missiles at them was transferred to nations in the August-September 2013 push for an attack on Syria—which was to be attacked as punishment for the alleged use of a banned weapon. But, of course, any ruler evil enough to have gassed hundreds to death would be unlikely to feel punished when hundreds more were killed, as he remained unhurt and unindicted.

The Really Good War in the Future

Of course, cataloging the wars that might have been replaced with dialogue or by altering policy goals can hardly persuade everyone that a war won't be needed in the future. The central belief in the minds of millions of people is this: One could not speak with Hitler. And its corollary: One cannot speak with the next Hitler. That the U.S. government has been misidentifying new Hitlers for three-quarters of a century—during which time many other nations have found the United States to be the nation you can't talk to—hardly addresses the notion that a Hitler *might* return some day. This theoretical danger is answered with incredible investment and energy, while dangers like global warming must, apparently, be proven to have already entered an unstoppable cycle of worsening catastrophe before we act.

I will address the great albatross of World War II in Section II of this book. It is, however, worth noting for now that three-quarters of a century is a long time. Much has changed. There has been no World War III. Wealthy armed nations of the world have not gone to war with each other again. Wars are fought among poor nations, with poor nations as proxies, or by wealthy nations against poor ones. Empires of the old variety have gone out of fashion, replaced by the new U.S. variation (military troops in 175 countries, but no colonies established). Small-time dictators may be very unpleasant, but none of them are planning world conquest. The United States has had an extremely difficult time occupying Iraq and Afghanistan. U.S.-backed rulers in Tunisia, Egypt, and Yemen have had a hard time suppressing nonviolent resistance by their people. Empires and tyrannies fail, and they fail more quickly than ever. The people of Eastern Europe who nonviolently got rid of the Soviet Union and their communist rulers will never be traded away to a new Hitler, and neither will any other nations' populations. The power of nonviolent resistance has become too well known. The idea of colonialism and empire has become too disreputable. The new Hitler will be more of a grotesque anachronism than an existential threat.

Small-Scale State Killing

Another venerable institution is going the way of the dodo. In the mid-eighteenth century proposing to eliminate the death penalty was widely considered dangerous and foolish. But most of the world's governments no longer use the death penalty. Among wealthy nations there is one exception remaining. The United States uses the death penalty and is, in fact, among the top five killers in the world—which isn't saying much in historical terms, the killing has dropped off so dramatically. Also in the top five: the recently "liberated" Iraq. But most of the United States' 50 states no longer use the death penalty. There are 18 states that have abolished it, including 6 thus far in the twenty-first century. Thirty-one states haven't used the death penalty in the past 5 years, 26 in the past 10 years, 17 in the past 40 years or more. A handful of Southern states— with Texas in the lead—do most of the killing. And all the killings combined amount to a small fraction of the rate at which the death penalty was used in the United States, adjusted for population, in previous centuries. Arguments for the death penalty are still easy to find, but they almost never claim that it can't be eliminated, only that it shouldn't be. Once considered critical to our security, the death penalty is now universally considered optional and widely considered archaic, counter-productive, and shameful. What if that were to happen to war?

Other Types of Violence Declining

Gone in some parts of the world, along with the death penalty, are all sorts of horrific public punishments and forms of torture and cruelty. Gone or reduced is a great deal of violence that was part of everyday life in centuries and decades gone by. Murder rates, in the long view, are declining dramatically. So are fist fights and beatings, violence toward spouses, violence toward children (by teachers and parents), violence toward animals, and public acceptance of all such violence. As anyone knows who tries to read to their children their own favorite books from childhood, it's not just the ancient fairy tales that are violent. Fist fights are as common as air in the books of our youth, not to mention classic movies. When Mr. Smith goes to Washington, Jimmy Stewart tries the filibuster only after punching everyone in sight fails to solve his problems. Magazine advertisements and television sit-coms in the 1950s joked about domestic violence. Such violence isn't gone, but its public acceptance is gone, and its reality is on the decline.

How can this be? Our underlying violence is supposed to be a justification for institutions like war. If our violence (at least in some forms) can be left behind us, along with sentiment about our alleged "human nature," why should an institution founded on belief in that violence remain?

What, after all, is "natural" about the violence of war? Most human or primate or mammalian conflicts within a species involve threats and bluffs and restraint. War involves an all-out attack on people you've never seen before. (Read Paul Chappell's books for excellent further discussion.) Those who cheer for war from a distance can romanticize its naturalness. But most people have nothing to do with it and want nothing to do with it. Are they unnatural? Are the majority of humans living outside "human nature"? Are you yourself an "unnatural" human because you don't fight wars?

Nobody has ever suffered post-traumatic stress disorder from war deprivation. Participation in war requires, for most people, intense training and conditioning. Killing others and facing others trying to kill you are both extremely difficult tasks that often leave one deeply damaged. In recent years, the U.S. military has been losing more soldiers to suicide in or after return from Afghanistan than to any other cause in that war. An estimated 20,000 members of the U.S. military have deserted during the first decade of the "global war on terror" (this according to Robert Fantina, author of *Desertion and the American Soldier*). We tell each other that the military is "voluntary." It was made "voluntary," not because so many people wanted to join, but because so many people hated the draft and wanted to avoid joining, and because propaganda and promises of financial reward could induce people to "volunteer." The volunteers are disproportionately people who had few other options available. And no volunteer in the U.S. military is permitted to quit volunteering.

Ideas Whose Time Has Come

In 1977 a campaign called the Hunger Project sought to eliminate world hunger. Success remains elusive. But most people today are convinced that hunger and starvation could be eliminated. In 1977, the Hunger Project felt obliged to argue against the widespread belief that hunger was inevitable. This was the text of a flyer they used:

> *Hunger is not inevitable.*
> *Everyone knows that people will always starve, the way everyone knew that man would never fly.*
> *At one time in human history, everyone knew that ...*
> *The world was flat,*
> *The sun revolved around the earth,*
> *Slavery was an economic necessity,*
> *A four-minute mile was impossible,*

Polio and smallpox would always be with us,
And no one would ever set foot on the moon.
Until courageous people challenged old beliefs and a new
idea's time had come.
All the forces in the world are not so powerful as an idea
whose time has come.

That last line is of course borrowed from Victor Hugo. He imagined a united Europe, but the time hadn't yet come. It later came. He imagined the abolition of war, but the time hadn't yet come. Perhaps now it has. Many didn't think land mines could be eliminated, yet that's well underway. Many thought nuclear war was inevitable and nuclear abolition impossible (for a long time the most radical demand was for a freeze in the creation of new weapons, not their elimination). Now nuclear abolition remains a distant goal, but most people admit that it can be done. The first step in abolishing war will be to recognize that it, too, is possible.

War Less Venerable Than Imagined

War is alleged to be "natural" (whatever that means) because it has supposedly always been around. The trouble is that it hasn't. In 200,000 years of human history and prehistory there is no evidence of war over 13,000 years old, and virtually none over 10,000 years old. (For those of you who believe the earth is only 6,500 years old, let me just say this: I've just spoken with God and he instructed us all to work for the abolition of war. He did, however, also recommend reading the rest of this book and purchasing many more copies.)

War is not common among nomads or hunters and gatherers. (See "Lethal Aggression in Mobile Forager Bands and Implications for the Origins of War," in *Science,* July 19, 2013.) Our species did not evolve with war. War belongs to complex sedentary societies— but only to some of them, and only some of the time. Belligerent societies grow peaceful and vice versa. In *Beyond War: The Human Potential for Peace,* Douglas Fry lists non-warring societies from all over the globe. Australia for some time before the Europeans came, the Arctic, Northeast Mexico, the Great Basin of North America—in these places people lived without war.

In 1614 Japan cut itself off from the West, and experienced peace, prosperity, and the blossoming of Japanese art and culture. In 1853 the U.S. Navy forced Japan open to U.S. merchants, missionaries, and militarism. Japan has done well with a peaceful Constitution since the end of World War II (although the United States is pushing hard for its repeal), as has Germany—apart from assisting NATO with its wars. Iceland and Sweden and Switzerland haven't fought their own wars in centuries, although they have assisted NATO in occupying Afghanistan. And NATO is busy now militarizing the north of Norway, Sweden, and Finland. Costa Rica abolished its military in 1948 and put it in a museum. Costa Rica has lived without war or military coups, in stark contrast to its neighbors, ever since—although it has assisted the United States' military, and although the militarism and weaponry of Nicaragua have spilled over. Costa Rica, far from perfect, is often ranked as the happiest or one of the happiest places to live on earth. In 2003 various nations had to be bribed or threatened to join in a "coalition" war on Iraq, and with many those efforts were unsuccessful.

In *The End of War,* John Horgan describes efforts to abolish war undertaken by members of an Amazonian tribe in the 1950s. Waorani villagers had been warring for years. A group of Waorani women and two missionaries decided to fly a small plane over hostile camps and deliver conciliatory messages from a loud speaker. Then there were face-to-face meetings. Then the wars ceased, to the great satisfaction of all concerned. The villagers did not return to war.

Who Fights the Most

As far as I know, nobody ranks nations based on their predilection to launch or participate in war. Fry's list of 70 or 80 peaceful nations includes nations that participate in NATO wars. The Global Peace Index (see VisionOfHumanity.org) ranks countries based on 22 factors including violent crime within the nation, political instability, etc. The United States ends up ranked in the middle, and European countries toward the top—that is, among the most "peaceful."

But the Global Peace Index website allows you to change the rankings by clicking only on the single factor of "conflicts fought." When you do this the United States ends up near the top—that is, among the nations engaged in the most conflicts. Why is it not at the very top, the "greatest purveyor of violence in the world," as Dr. Martin Luther King Jr. called it? Because the United States is ranked based on the idea that it has engaged in only three conflicts during the past 5 years—this despite drone wars in several nations, military operations in dozens, and troops stationed in some 175 and climbing. Thus the United States is outranked by three nations with four conflicts each: India, Myanmar, and the Democratic Republic of the Congo. Even by this crude measurement, however, what jumps out at you is that the vast majority of nations—virtually every nation on earth—is less involved in war making than the United States is, and many nations have not known war the past five years, while many nations' only conflict has been a coalition war led by the United States and in which other nations played or are playing small parts.

Follow the Money

The Global Peace Index (GPI) ranks the United States near the peaceful end of the scale on the factor of military spending. It accomplishes this feat through two tricks. First, the GPI lumps the majority of the world's nations all the way at the extreme peaceful end of the spectrum rather than distributing them evenly.

Second, the GPI treats military spending as a percentage of gross domestic product (GDP) or the size of an economy. This suggests that a rich country with a huge military can be more peaceful than a poor country with a small military. Perhaps that is so in terms of intentions, but it is not so in terms of results. Is it necessarily even so in terms of intentions? One country desires a certain level of killing machinery and is willing to forego more to get it. The other country desires that same level of military plus much more, although the sacrifice is in a certain sense less. If that wealthier country becomes even wealthier but refrains from building an even bigger military purely because it can afford to, has it become less militaristic or remained the same? This is not just an academic question, as think tanks in Washington urge spending a higher percentage of GDP on the military, exactly as if one should invest more in warfare whenever possible, without waiting for a defensive need.

In contrast to the GPI, the Stockholm International Peace Research Institute (SIPRI) lists the United States as the top military spender in the world, measured in dollars spent. In fact, according to SIPRI, the United States spends as much on war and war preparation as most of the rest of the world combined. The truth may be more dramatic still. SIPRI says U.S. military spending in 2011 was $711 billion. Chris Hellman of the National Priorities Project says it was $1,200 billion, or $1.2 trillion. The difference comes from including military spending found in every department of the government, not just "Defense," but also Homeland Security, State, Energy, the U.S. Agency for International Development, the Central Intelligence Agency, the National Security Agency, the Veterans Administration, interest on war debts, etc. There's no way to do an apples-to-apples comparison to other nations without accurate credible information on each nation's total military spending, but it is extremely safe to assume that no other nation on earth is spending $500 billion more than is listed for it in the SIPRI rankings. Moreover, some of the biggest military spenders after the United States are U.S. allies and NATO members. And many of the big and small spenders are actively encouraged to spend, and to spend on U.S. weaponry, by the U.S. State Department and the U.S. military.

While North Korea almost certainly spends a much higher percentage of its gross domestic product on war preparations than the United States does, it almost certainly spends less than 1 percent what the United States spends. Who is therefore more violent is one question, perhaps unanswerable. Who is more of a threat to whom is no question at all. With no nation threatening the United States, the Directors of National Intelligence in recent years have had a hard time telling Congress who the enemy is and have identified the enemy in various reports merely as "extremists."

The point of comparing levels of military spending is not that we should be ashamed of how evil the United States is, or proud of how exceptional. Rather, the point is that decreased militarism is not only humanly possible; it is being practiced right now by every other nation on earth, that is to say: nations containing 96 percent of humanity. The United States spends the most on its military, keeps the most troops stationed in the most countries, engages in the most conflicts, sells the most weaponry to others, and thumbs its nose most blatantly at the use of courts to restrain its war-making or even, any more, to put individuals on trial who can just as easily be hit with a hellfire missile. Lessening U.S. militarism would not violate some law of "human nature," but bring the United States more closely into line with most of humanity.

Public Opinion v. War

Militarism is not nearly as popular in the United States as the behavior of the U.S. government would suggest to someone who believed the government followed the will of the people. In

2011, the media made a lot of noise about a budget crisis and did a lot of polling on how to solve it. Almost nobody (single-digit percentages in some polls) was interested in the solutions the government was interested in: cutting Social Security and Medicare. But the second most popular solution, after taxing the rich, was consistently cutting the military. According to Gallup polling, a plurality has believed the U.S. government is spending too much on the military since 2003. And, according to polling, including by Rasmussen, as well as according to my own experience, virtually everyone underestimates how much the United States is spending. Only a small minority in the United States believes the U.S. government should spend three times as much as any other nation on its military. Yet the United States has spent well over that level for years, even as measured by SIPRI. The Program for Public Consultation (PPC), affiliated with the School of Public Policy at the University of Maryland, has tried to correct for ignorance. First PPC shows people what the actual public budget looks like. Then it asks what they would change. A majority favors major cuts to the military.

Even when it comes to specific wars, the U.S. public is not as supportive as sometimes thought by U.S. people themselves or by citizens of other countries, especially countries invaded by the United States. The Vietnam Syndrome much lamented in Washington for decades was not an illness caused by Agent Orange but rather a name for popular opposition to wars—as if that opposition were a disease. In 2012, President Obama announced a 13-year, $65-million project to commemorate (and rehabilitate the reputation of) the war on Vietnam. The U.S. public has opposed

U.S. wars on Syria or Iran for years. Of course that could change the minute such a war is launched. There was significant public support at first for the invasions of Afghanistan and Iraq. But fairly quickly that opinion shifted. For years, a strong majority favored ending those wars and believed it had been a mistake to begin them—while the wars rolled "successfully" along in the supposed cause of "spreading democracy." The 2011 war on Libya was opposed by the United Nations (whose resolution did not authorize a war to overthrow the government), by the U.S. Congress (but why worry over that technicality!), and by the U.S. public (see PollingReport. com/libya.htm). In September 2013, the public and the Congress rejected a major push by the president for an attack on Syria.

Human Hunting

When we say that war goes back 10,000 years it's not clear that we're talking about a single thing, as opposed to two or more different things going by the same name. Picture a family in Yemen or Pakistan living under a constant buzz produced by a drone overhead. One day their home and everyone in it is shattered by a missile. Were they at war? Where was the battlefield? Where were their weapons? Who declared the war? What was contested in the war? How would it end?

Let's take the case of someone actually engaged in anti-U.S. terrorism. He's struck by a missile from an unseen unmanned airplane and killed. Was he at war in a sense that a Greek or Roman warrior would recognize? How about a warrior in an early modern war? Would someone who thinks of a war as requiring a battlefield and combat between two armies recognize a drone warrior seated at his desk manipulating his computer joystick as a warrior at all?

Like dueling, war has formerly been thought of as an agreed upon contest between two rational actors. Two groups agreed, or at least their rulers agreed, to go to war. Now war is always marketed as a last resort. Wars are always fought for "peace," while nobody ever makes peace for the sake of war. War is presented as an undesired means toward some nobler end, an unfortunate responsibility required by the irrationality of the other side. Now that other side is not fighting on a literal battlefield; rather the side equipped with satellite technology is hunting the supposed fighters.

The drive behind this transformation has not been the technology itself or military strategy, but public opposition to putting U.S. troops on a battlefield. That same repulsion toward losing "our own boys" was largely what led to the Vietnam Syndrome. Such repulsion fueled opposition to the wars on Iraq and Afghanistan. Most Americans had and still have no idea about the extent of the death and suffering borne by people on the other sides of the wars. (The government is disinclined to inform people, who have been known to respond very appropriately.) It's true that U.S. people haven't consistently insisted that their government present them with information on the suffering caused by U.S. wars. Many, to the extent that they do know, have been more tolerant of the pain of foreigners. But the deaths and injuries to U.S. troops have become largely intolerable. This partially accounts for the recent U.S. move toward air wars and drone wars.

The question is whether a drone war is a war at all. If it's fought by robots against which the other side has no ability to respond, how closely does it resemble most of what we categorize in human history as war-making? Is it not perhaps the case that we have already ended war and now must end something else as well (a name for it might be: *the hunting of humans*, or if you prefer *assassination*, although that tends to suggest the killing of a public figure)? And then, wouldn't the task of ending that other thing present us with a much less venerable institution to dismantle?

Both institutions, war and human hunting, involve the killing of foreigners. The new one involves the intentional killing of U.S. citizens as well, but the old one involved the killing of U.S. traitors or deserters. Still, if we can change our manner of killing foreigners to render it almost unrecognizable, who's to say we can't eliminate the practice altogether?

Do We Have No Choice?

Although we might each individually be free to choose to end war (a different question from whether you do at the moment choose to) is there some inevitability that prevents us from making that choice together collectively? There wasn't when it came to chattel slavery, blood feuds, duels, capital punishment, child labor, tar and feathering, the stocks and pillory, wives as chattel, the punishment of homosexuality, or countless other institutions past or quickly passing—although for many years in each case it *seemed* impossible to dismantle the practice. It is certainly true that people often collectively act in a manner opposed to how a majority of them each individually claim they would like to act. (I've even seen a poll in which a majority of CEOs claim they'd like to be taxed more.) But there is no evidence that collective failure is inevitable. The suggestion that war is different from other institutions that have been eliminated is an empty suggestion unless some concrete claim is made as to *how* we are prevented from ending it.

John Horgan's *The End of War* is well worth reading. A writer for *Scientific American,* Horgan approaches the question of whether war can be ended as a scientist. After extensive research, he concludes that war can be ended globally and has in various times and places been ended. Before reaching that conclusion, Horgan examines claims to the contrary.

While our wars are advertised as humanitarian expeditions or defenses against evil threats, and not as competition for resources, such as fossil fuels, some scientists who argue for war's inevitability tend to assume that war is in fact competition for fossil fuels. Many citizens agree with that analysis and support or oppose the wars on that basis. Such an explanation for our wars is clearly incomplete, as they always have numerous motivations. But if we accept the claim for the sake of argument that current wars are for oil and gas, what can we make of the argument that they are inevitable?

The argument holds that humans have always competed, and that when resources are scarce war results. But even proponents of this theory admit that they are not really claiming inevitability. If we were to control population growth and/or shift to green energy and/or alter our consumption habits, the supposedly necessary resources of oil and gas and coal would no longer be in scarce supply, and our violent competition for them would no longer be inevitable.

Looking through history we see examples of wars that seem to fit the model of resource pressure and others that don't. We see societies burdened by resource scarcity that turn to war and others that do not. We also see cases of war as a cause of scarcity, rather than the reverse. Horgan cites examples of peoples who fought most when resources were most plentiful. Horgan also cites the work of anthropologists Carol and Melvin Ember whose study of over 360 societies over the past two centuries turned up no correlation between resource scarcity or population density and war. Lewis Fry Richardson's similarly massive study also found no such correlation.

In other words, the story that population growth or resource scarcity causes war is a just-so story. It makes a certain logical sense. Elements of the story have in fact been part of the narrative of many wars. But the evidence indicates that there is nothing there in the way of a necessary or sufficient cause. These factors do not make war inevitable. If a particular society *decides* that it will fight for scarce resources, then the depletion of those resources makes that society more likely to go to war. That is indeed a real danger for us. But there is nothing inevitable about the society's making the decision that some type of event will justify a war in the first place, or acting on that decision when the time arrives.

Puppets of Sociopaths?

What about the idea that certain individuals dedicated to war will inevitably drag the rest of us into it? I've argued above that our government is more eager for war than our population. Do those who favor war overlap heavily with those who hold positions of power? And does this condemn us all to war-making whether we want it or not?

Let's be clear, first of all, that there is nothing strictly inevitable about such a claim. Those war-prone individuals could be identified and altered or controlled. Our system of government, including our system of funding elections and our system of communications, could be altered. Our system of government, in fact, originally planned for no standing armies and gave war powers to Congress for fear that any president would abuse them. In the 1930s Congress almost gave war powers to the public by requiring a referendum before a war. Congress has now given war powers to presidents, but that need not be permanently so. Indeed, in September 2013, Congress stood up to the president on Syria.

In addition, let's keep in mind that war is not unique as an issue on which our government diverges from majority opinion. On many other topics the divergence is at least as pronounced, if not more so: the bailing out of banks, the surveillance of the public, the subsidies for billionaires and corporations, the corporate trade agreements, the secret laws, the failure to protect the environment. There are not dozens of urges overpowering the public will through the power-grabbing of sociopaths. Rather, there are sociopaths and non-sociopaths falling under the influence of good old-fashioned corruption.

The 2 percent of the population who, studies suggest, fully enjoy killing in war and do not suffer from it, do not move from euphoria to remorse (see Dave Grossman's *On Killing*), probably do not overlap much with those in power making decisions to fight wars. Our political leaders do not take part in wars themselves anymore and in many cases evaded wars in their youth. Their drive to power may lead them to attempt greater domination through warfare fought by subordinates, but it wouldn't do so in a culture in which peace-making increased one's power more than war-making did.

In my book, *When the World Outlawed War,* I told the story of the creation of the Kellogg-Briand Pact, which banned war in 1928 (it's still on the books!). Frank Kellogg, the U.S. Secretary of State, was as supportive of war as anyone else until it became clear to him that peace was the direction for career advancement. He began telling his wife he might win the Nobel Peace Prize, which he did. He began thinking he might become a judge on the International Court of Justice, which he did. He began responding to the demands of peace activists he had earlier denounced. A generation earlier or later, Kellogg would probably have pursued war-making as the path to power. In the anti-war climate of his day he saw a different route.

The All-Powerful Military Industrial Complex

When war is viewed as something done exclusively by non-Americans or non-Westerners, the alleged causes of war include theories about genetics, population density, resource scarcity, etc. John Horgan is right to point out that these alleged causes don't make war inevitable and don't in fact correlate with the likelihood of war.

When war is understood as also, if not primarily, something done by "developed" nations, then other causes emerge that Horgan never looked at. These causes also bring no inevitability with them. But they can make war more likely in a culture that has made certain choices. It's critical that we recognize and understand these factors, because a movement to abolish war will have to address itself to war making by the United States and its allies in a manner different from what would seem appropriate if war were exclusively a product of the poor nations in Africa where the International Criminal Court manages to find virtually all of its cases.

In addition to being immersed in a false world view of war's inevitability, people in the United States are up against corrupt elections, complicit media, shoddy education, slick propaganda, insidious entertainment, and a gargantuan permanent war machine falsely presented as a necessary economic program that cannot be dismantled. But none of this is unalterable. We're dealing here with forces that make war more likely in our time and place, not insurmountable obstacles that guarantee war forevermore. No one believes the military industrial complex has always been with us. And with a little reflection no one would believe that, like global warming, it could create a feedback loop outside of human control. On the contrary, the MIC exists through its influence on humans. It didn't always exist. It expands and contracts. It lasts as long as we allow it to. The military industrial complex is, in short, optional, just as the chattel slavery complex was optional.

In later sections of this book we'll discuss what can be done about a cultural acceptance of war that draws less on population growth or resource scarcity than on patriotism, xenophobia, the sad state of journalism, and the political influence of companies like Lockheed Martin. Understanding this will allow us to shape an anti-war movement more likely to succeed. Its success is not guaranteed, but it is without any doubt possible.

"We Can't End War If They Don't End War"

There is an important difference between slavery (and many other institutions) on the one hand, and war on the other. If one group of people makes war on another, then both are at war. If Canada developed slave plantations, the United States wouldn't have to do so. If Canada invaded the United States, the two nations *would* be at war. This would seem to suggest that war must be eliminated everywhere simultaneously. Otherwise, the need for defense against others must keep war alive forever.

This argument ultimately fails on several grounds. For one thing, the contrast between war and slavery is not as simple as suggested. If Canada were using slavery, guess where Wal-Mart would start importing our stuff from! If Canada were using slavery, guess what Congress would be setting up commissions to study the benefits of reestablishing! Any institution can be contagious, even if perhaps less so than war.

Also, the argument above is not for war so much as for defense against war. If Canada attacked the United States, the world could sanction the Canadian government, put its leaders on trial, and shame the entire nation. Canadians could refuse to participate in their government's war-making. Americans could refuse to recognize the authority of the foreign occupation. Others could travel to the United States to aid the nonviolent resistance. Like the Danes under the Nazis, we could refuse to cooperate. So, there are tools of defense other than the military.

(I apologize to Canada for this hypothetical example. I am, in fact, aware which of our two countries has a history of invading the other [See DavidSwanson.org/node/4125].)

But let's suppose some military defense was still believed necessary. Would it have to be $1 trillion worth each year? Wouldn't U.S. defense needs be similar to the defense needs of other nations? Let's suppose the enemy is not Canada, but a band of international terrorists. Would this change the needs for military defense? Perhaps, but not in a manner to justify $1 trillion per year. The nuclear arsenal of the United States did nothing to dissuade the 9/11 terrorists. The permanent stationing of a million soldiers in some 175 nations doesn't help prevent terrorism. Rather, as discussed below, it provokes it. It may help us to ask ourselves this question: Why is Canada not the target of terrorism that the United States is?

Ending militarism need not take many years, but it also need not be instantaneous or globally coordinated. The United States is the leading exporter of weapons to other nations. That can't be very easily justified in terms of national defense. (An obvious actual motive is money making.) Ending U.S. weapon exportation could be accomplished without impacting the United States' own defenses. Advances in international law, justice, and arbitration could combine with advances in disarmament and foreign aid, and with a growing global cultural revulsion against war. Terrorism could be treated as the crime that it is, its provocation reduced, and its commission prosecuted in court with greater international cooperation. A reduction in terrorism and in war (a.k.a. state terrorism) could lead to further disarmament, and the limiting and ultimate elimination of the profit motive from war. Successful nonviolent arbitration of disputes could lead to greater reliance on and compliance with the law. As we'll see in Section IV of this book, a process could be begun that would move the world away from war, the world's nations away from militarism, and the world's enraged individuals away from terrorism. It is simply not the case that we must prepare for war out of fear that someone else might attack us. Nor must we abolish all tools of war by next Thursday in order to commit to never fighting a war again.

It's in Our Heads

Here in the United States, war is in our heads, and our books, our movies, our toys, our games, our historical markers, our monuments, our sporting events, our wardrobes, our television advertisements. When he searched for a correlation between war and some other factor, Horgan only found one factor. Wars are made by cultures that celebrate or tolerate war. War is an idea that spreads itself. It is indeed contagious. And it serves its own ends, not those of its hosts (outside of certain profiteers).

The anthropologist Margaret Mead called war a cultural invention. It is a kind of cultural contagion. Wars happen because of cultural acceptance, and they can be avoided by cultural rejection. The anthropologist Douglas Fry, in his first book on this subject, *The Human Potential for Peace*, describes societies that reject war. Wars are not created by genes or avoided by eugenics or oxytocin. Wars are not driven by an ever-present minority of sociopaths or avoided by controlling them. Wars are not made inevitable by resource scarcity or inequality or prevented by prosperity and shared wealth. Wars are not determined by the weaponry available or the influence of the profiteers. All such factors play parts in wars, but none of them can make wars *inevitable*. The decisive factor is a militaristic culture, a culture that glorifies war or even just accepts it (and you can accept something even while telling a pollster you oppose it; real opposition takes work). War spreads as other memes spread, culturally. The abolition of war can do the same.

A Sartrean thinker arrives at more or less this same conclusion (not that war should be abolished but that it *could* be) without Fry's or Horgan's research. I think the research is helpful for those who need it. But there is a weakness. As long as we rely on such research, we must remain concerned that some new scientific or anthropological study could come along to prove that war is in fact in our genes. We should not get into the habit of imagining that we must wait for authorities to prove to us that something has been done in the past before we attempt to do it. Other authorities could come along and disprove it.

Instead, we should come to a clear understanding that even if no society had ever existed without war, ours could be the first. People invest great effort in creating wars. They could choose not to do so. Transforming this glaringly obvious observation into a scientific study of whether enough people have rejected war in the past to reject it in the future is both helpful and harmful to the cause. It helps those who need to see that what they want to do has been done before. It hurts collective development of innovative imagining.

Mistaken theories about the causes of war create the self-fulfilling expectation that war will always be with us. Predicting that climate change will produce world war may actually fail to inspire people to demand a sane public energy policy, inspiring them instead to support military spending and to stock up on guns and emergency supplies. Up until a war is launched it is not inevitable, but preparing for wars does indeed make them more likely. (See *Tropic of Chaos: Climate Change and the New Geography of Violence* by Christian Parenti.)

Studies have found that when people are exposed to the idea that they have no "free will" they behave less morally. (See "The Value of Believing in Free Will: Encouraging a Belief in Determinism Increases Cheating," by Kathleen D. Vohs and Jonathan W. Schooler in *Psychological Science,* Volume 19, Number 1.) Who could blame them? They "had no free will." But the fact that all physical behavior may be predetermined doesn't change the fact that *from my perspective* I will always appear free, and choosing to behave badly will remain just as inexcusable even if a philosopher or scientist confuses me into thinking I have no choice. If we are misled into believing that war is inevitable, we will think we can hardly be blamed for launching wars. But we will be wrong. Choosing evil behavior always deserves blame.

But Why Is It in Our Heads?

If the cause of war is the cultural acceptance of war, what are the causes of that acceptance? There are possible rational causes, such as misinformation and ignorance produced by schools and news media and entertainment, including ignorance of the harm wars do and ignorance regarding nonviolence as an alternative form of conflict. There are possible non-rational causes, such as poor care of infants and young children, insecurity, xenophobia, racism, subservience, ideas about masculinity, greed, lack of community, apathy, etc. There may, therefore, be root contributors (not strictly necessary or sufficient causes) of war to be addressed. There may be more to do than making a rational argument against war. That does not mean, however, that any of the contributors is itself inevitable, or that it is a sufficient cause for war-making.

II. WAR SHOULD BE ENDED

While most people don't believe that war *can* be ended (and I hope Section I of this book begins ever so slightly to change some minds), many also don't believe that war *should* be ended. Of course it's easier to dismiss the question of whether war should be ended if you've decided that it can't be ended, just as it's easier not to worry about the possibility of ending it if you've decided that it should be maintained. So, the two beliefs are mutually supporting. Both are mistaken, and weakening one helps to weaken the other, but both run deep in our culture. There are even some people who believe that war can and should be abolished, but who propose using war as the tool with which to do the job. That confusion illustrates just how difficult it is for us to arrive at a position in favor of abolition.

"Defense" Endangers Us

Since 1947, when the Department of War was renamed the Department of Defense, the U.S. military has been on the offensive at least as much as always. Assaults on Native Americans, the Philippines, Latin America, etc., by the War Department had not been defensive; and neither were the Defense Department's wars in Korea, Vietnam, Iraq, etc. While the best defense in many sports may be a good offense, an offense in war is not defensive, not when it generates hatred, resentment, and blowback, not when the alternative is no war at all. Through the course of the so-called global war on terrorism, terrorism has been on the rise.

This was predictable and predicted. People outraged by attacks and occupations just weren't going to be eliminated or won over by more attacks and occupations. Pretending that they "hate our freedoms," as President George W. Bush claimed, or that they just have the wrong religion or are completely irrational doesn't change this. Pursuing legal recourse by prosecuting those responsible for the crimes of mass-murder on 9/11 might have helped to deter additional terrorism better than launching wars. It also wouldn't hurt for the U.S. government to stop arming dictators (as I write this, the Egyptian military is attacking Egyptian civilians with weapons provided by the United States, and the White House is refusing to cut off the "aid," meaning weapons), defending crimes against Palestinians (try reading *The General's Son* by Miko Peled), and stationing U.S. troops in other people's countries. The wars on Iraq and Afghanistan, and the abuses of prisoners during them, became major recruiting tools for anti-U.S. terrorism.

In 2006, U.S. intelligence agencies produced a National Intelligence Estimate that reached just that conclusion. The Associated Press reported: "The war in Iraq has become a *cause célèbre* for Islamic extremists, breeding deep resentment of the U.S. that probably will get worse before it gets better, federal intelligence analysts conclude in a report at odds with President Bush's contention of a world growing safer. ... [T]he nation's most veteran analysts conclude that despite serious damage to the leadership of al-Qaida, the threat from Islamic extremists has spread both in numbers and in geographic reach."

The extent to which the U.S. government pursues counter-terrorism policies that it knows will generate terrorism has led many to conclude that reducing terrorism is not a big priority, and some to conclude that generating terrorism is in fact the goal. Leah Bolger, a former president of Veterans For Peace, says, "the U.S. government *knows* that the wars are counter-productive, that is, *if* your purpose is to reduce the number of 'terrorists.' But the purpose of American wars is not to make peace, it is to make more enemies so that we can continue the endless cycle of war."

Now comes the part where it indeed gets worse before better. There is a new top recruiting tool: drone strikes and targeted killings. Veterans of U.S. kill teams in Iraq and Afghanistan interviewed in Jeremy Scahill's book and film *Dirty Wars* said that whenever they worked their way through a list of people to kill, they were handed a larger list; the list grew as a result of working their way through it. General Stanley McChrystal, then commander of U.S. and NATO forces in Afghanistan told *Rolling Stone* in June 2010 that "for every innocent person you kill, you create 10 new enemies." The Bureau of Investigative Journalism and others have meticulously documented the names of many innocents killed by drone strikes.

In 2013, McChrystal said there was widespread resentment against drone strikes in Pakistan. According to the Pakistani newspaper *Dawn* on February 10, 2013, McChrystal, "warned that too many drone strikes in Pakistan without identifying suspected militants individually can be a bad thing. Gen. McChrystal said he understood why Pakistanis, even in the areas not affected by the drones, reacted negatively against the strikes. He asked the Americans how they would react if a neighbouring country like Mexico started firing drone missiles at targets in Texas. The Pakistanis, he said, saw the drones as a demonstration of America's might against their nation and reacted accordingly. 'What scares me about drone strikes is how they are perceived around the world,' Gen. McChrystal said in an earlier interview. 'The resentment created by American use of unmanned strikes ... is much greater than the average American appreciates. They are hated on a visceral level, even by people who've never seen one or seen the effects of one.'"

As early as 2010, Bruce Riedel, who coordinated a review of Afghanistan policy for President Obama said, "The pressure we've put on [jihadist forces] in the past year has also drawn them together, meaning that the network of alliances is growing stronger not weaker." (*New York Times,* May 9, 2010.) Former Director of National Intelligence Dennis Blair said that while "drone attacks did help reduce the Qaeda leadership in Pakistan, they also increased hatred of America" and damaged "our ability to work with Pakistan [in] eliminating Taliban sanctuaries, encouraging Indian-Pakistani dialogue, and making Pakistan's nuclear arsenal more secure." (*New York Times,* August 15, 2011.)

Michael Boyle, part of Obama's counter-terrorism group during his 2008 election campaign, says the use of drones is having "adverse strategic effects that have not been properly weighed against the tactical gains associated with killing terrorists. ... The vast increase in the number of deaths of low-ranking operatives has deepened political resistance to the US programme in Pakistan, Yemen and other countries." (*The Guardian,* January 7, 2013.) "We're seeing that blowback. If you're trying to kill your way to a solution, no matter how precise you are, you're going to upset people even if they're not targeted," echoed Gen. James E. Cartwright, the former vice chairman of the Joint Chiefs of Staff. (*The New York Times,* March 22, 2013.)

These views are not uncommon. The CIA's station chief in Islamabad in 2005-2006 thought the drone strikes, then still infrequent, had "done little except fuel hatred for the United States inside Pakistan." (See *The Way of the Knife* by Mark Mazzetti.) The top U.S. civilian official in part of Afghanistan, Matthew Hoh, resigned in protest and commented, "I think we're engendering more hostility. We're wasting a lot of very good assets going after midlevel guys who don't threaten the United States or have no capacity to threaten the United States." For many more such viewpoints see Fred Branfman's collection at WarIsACrime.org/LessSafe.

An Unusual Hearing With Something to Be Heard

In April 2013, a U.S. Senate Judiciary subcommittee held a hearing on drones that it had previously delayed. As it happened, during the delay, the home town of one of the scheduled witnesses was struck by a drone. Farea al-Muslimi, a young man from Yemen, described "an attack that terrified thousands of simple, poor farmers."

Al-Muslimi said, "I have visited locations where U.S. targeted killing strikes have hit their intended targets. And I have visited sites where the U.S. strikes missed their targets and instead killed or injured innocent civilians. I have spoken with grieving family members and angry villagers. I have seen Al Qaeda in the Arabian Peninsula (AQAP) use U.S. strikes to promote its agenda and try to recruit more terrorists."

Al-Muslimi detailed some of these cases. He also explained his gratitude to the United States for scholarships and an experience as an exchange student that allowed him to see more of the world than his tiny Yemeni village of Wessab. "For almost all of the people in Wessab," al-Muslimi said, "I'm the only person with any connection to the United States. They called and texted me that night with questions that I could not answer: Why was the United States terrifying them with these drones? Why was the United States trying to kill a person with a missile when everyone knows where he is and he could have been easily arrested?"

After the strike, the farmers in Wessab were afraid and angry. They were upset because they know Al-Radmi but they did not know that he was a target, so they could have potentially been with him during the missile strike. ...
In the past, most of Wessab's villagers knew little about the United States. My stories about my experiences in America, my American friends, and the American values that I saw for myself helped the villagers I talked to understand the America that I know and love. Now, however, when they think of America they think of the terror they feel from the drones that hover over their heads ready to fire missiles at any time. ...

> *There is nothing villagers in Wessab needed more than a school to educate the local children or a hospital to help decrease the number of women and children dying every day. Had the United States built a school or hospital, it would have instantly changed the lives of my fellow villagers for the better and been the most effective counterterrorism tool. And I can almost certainly assure you that the villagers would have gone to arrest the target themselves. ...*
>
> *What radicals had previously failed to achieve in my village, one drone strike accomplished in an instant: there is now an intense anger and growing hatred of America.*

Al-Muslimi arrived at the same conclusion that one hears from countless people, including top U.S. officials, in Pakistan and Yemen:

> *The killing of innocent civilians by U.S. missiles in Yemen is helping to destabilize my country and create an environment from which AQAP benefits. Every time an innocent civilian is killed or maimed by a U.S. drone strike or another targeted killing, it is felt by Yemenis across the country. These strikes often cause animosity towards the United States and create a backlash that undermines the national security goals of the United States.*

When Is Murder Not Murder?

Farea al-Muslimi's testimony was an unusually intense dose of reality in the halls of Congress. The rest of the witnesses in that hearing and most other hearings on the topic were law professors chosen for their unreserved approval of the drone kill program. A professor expected to approve of drone kills in Afghanistan but to oppose them as illegal in Pakistan, Yemen, Somalia, and elsewhere "outside the war zone," was stricken from the witness list. While the United Nations is "investigating" the illegality of drone strikes, the closest the senators came to hearing that viewpoint in the hearing at which al-Muslimi spoke came in the testimony of law professor Rosa Brooks.

The White House had refused to send any witnesses, as it had refused for various other hearings on the same topic. So Congress made do with law professors. But the law professors testified that, due to White House secrecy, they were incapable of knowing anything. Rosa Brooks testified, in effect, that drone strikes outside of an accepted war zone could be "murder" (her word) or they could be perfectly acceptable. The question was whether they were part of a war. If they were part of a war then they were perfectly acceptable. If they were not part of a war then they were murder. But the White House was claiming to have secret memos "legalizing" the drone strikes, and Brooks could not know without seeing the memos whether the memos said the drone strikes were part of a war or not.

Think about this for a minute. In this same room, at this same table, is Farea al-Muslimi, afraid to visit his mother, his heart bleeding for the terror inflicted on his village. And here comes a law professor to explain that it's all in perfect harmony with U.S. values as long as the President has put the right words down on a secret law that he won't show the U.S. people.

It's odd that murder is the only crime that war erases. Believers in civilized warfare maintain that, even in war, you cannot kidnap or rape or torture or steal or lie under oath or cheat on your taxes. But if you want to murder, that'll be just fine. Believers in uncivilized war find this hard to grasp. If you can murder, which is the worst thing possible, then why in the world—they ask—can you not torture a little bit too?

What is the substantive difference between being at war and not being at war, such that in one case an action is honorable and in the other it's murder? By definition, there is nothing substantive about it. If a secret memo can legalize drone kills by explaining that they are part of a war, then the difference is not substantive or observable. We cannot see it here in the heart of the empire, and al-Muslimi cannot see it in his drone-struck village in Yemen. The difference is something that can be contained in a secret memo. To tolerate war and live with ourselves, the majority of members of a community must engage in this moral blindness.

The results are not so secret. Micah Zenko of the Council on Foreign Relations wrote in January 2013, "There appears to be a strong correlation in Yemen between increased targeted killings since December 2009 and heightened anger toward the United States and sympathy with or allegiance to AQAP. ... One former senior military official closely involved in U.S. targeted killings argued that 'drone strikes are just a signal of arrogance that will boomerang against America. ... A world characterized by the proliferation of armed drones ... would undermine core U.S. interests, such as preventing armed conflict, promoting human rights, and strengthening international legal regimes.' Because of drones' inherent advantages over other weapons platforms, states and nonstate actors would be much more likely to use lethal force against the United States and its allies."

Our government has given this disastrous idea a name and is seeking to spread it far and wide. Gregory Johnson wrote in the *New York Times* on November 19, 2012: "The most enduring policy legacy of the past four years may well turn out to be an approach to counterterrorism that American officials call the 'Yemen model,' a mixture of drone strikes and Special Forces raids targeting Al Qaeda leaders. ... Testimonies from Qaeda fighters and interviews I and local journalists have conducted across Yemen attest to the centrality of civilian casualties in explaining Al Qaeda's rapid growth there. The United States is killing women, children and members of key tribes. 'Each time they kill a tribesman, they create more fighters for Al Qaeda,' one Yemeni explained to me over tea in Sana, the capital, last month. Another told *CNN*, after a failed strike, 'I would not be surprised if a hundred tribesmen joined Al Qaeda as a result of the latest drone mistake.'"

Who Would Carry Out Such Disastrous Policies?

A partial answer is: people who obey too readily, trust their supervisors excessively, and feel deep remorse when they stop and think. On June 6, 2013, *NBC News* interviewed a former drone pilot named Brandon Bryant who was deeply depressed over his role in killing over 1,600 people:

Brandon Bryant says he was sitting in a chair at a Nevada Air Force base operating the camera when his team fired two missiles from their drone at three men walking down a road halfway around the world in Afghanistan. The missiles hit all three targets, and Bryant says he could see the aftermath on his computer screen—including thermal images of a growing puddle of hot blood.

'The guy that was running forward, he's missing his right leg,' he recalled. 'And I watch this guy bleed out and, I mean, the blood is hot.' As the man died his body grew cold, said Bryant, and his thermal image changed until he became the same color as the ground.

'I can see every little pixel,' said Bryant, who has been diagnosed with post-traumatic stress disorder, 'if I just close my eyes.'

'People say that drone strikes are like mortar attacks,' Bryant said. 'Well, artillery doesn't see this. Artillery doesn't see the results of their actions. It's really more intimate for us, because we see everything.' ...

He's still not certain whether the three men in Afghanistan were really Taliban insurgents or just men with guns in a country where many people carry guns. The men were five miles from American forces arguing with each other when the first missile hit them. ...

He also remembers being convinced that he had seen a child scurry onto his screen during one mission just before a missile struck, despite assurances from others that the figure he'd seen was really a dog.

After participating in hundreds of missions over the years, Bryant said he 'lost respect for life' and began to feel like a sociopath. ...

In 2011, as Bryant's career as a drone operator neared its end, he said his commander presented him with what amounted to a scorecard. It showed that he had participated in missions that contributed to the deaths of 1,626 people.

'I would've been happy if they never even showed me the piece of paper,' he said. 'I've seen American soldiers die, innocent people die, and insurgents die. And it's not pretty. It's not something that I want to have—this diploma.'

Now that he's out of the Air Force and back home in Montana, Bryant said he doesn't want to think about how many people on that list might've been innocent: 'It's too heartbreaking.' ...

When he told a woman he was seeing that he'd been a drone operator, and contributed to the deaths of a large number of people, she cut him off. 'She looked at me like I was a monster,' he said. 'And she never wanted to touch me again.'

We're Endangering Others Too,
Not Protecting Them

Wars are packaged in falsehoods with such consistency (see my book *War Is A Lie*) largely because their promoters want to appeal to good and noble motivations. They say a war will defend us against a nonexistent threat, like the weapons in Iraq, because an open war of aggression wouldn't be approved of—and because fear and nationalism make many people eager to believe the falsehoods. There's nothing wrong with defense, after all. Who could possibly be against defense?

Or they say that a war will defend helpless people in Libya or Syria or some other country from dangers they are facing. We must bomb them to protect them. We have a "Responsibility to Protect." If someone is committing genocide, surely we should not stand by and watch when we could stop it.

But, as we've seen above, our wars endanger us rather than defending us. They endanger others too. They take bad situations and make them worse. Should we stop genocides? Of course, we should, if we can. But we shouldn't use wars to make the people of a suffering nation even worse off. In September 2013, President Obama urged everyone to watch videos of children dying in Syria, the implication being that if you care about those children you must support bombing Syria.

In fact, many war opponents, to their shame, argued that the United States should worry about its own children and stop shouldering the responsibilities of the world. But making things worse in a foreign country by bombing it is not anyone's responsibility; it's a crime. And it would not be improved by getting more nations to help with it.

So What Should We Do?

Well, first of all, we should create a world in which such horrors are not likely to occur (see Section IV of this book). Crimes such as genocide do not have justifications, but they do have causes, and there is usually plenty of warning.

Second, nations like the United States should adopt an even-handed policy toward human rights abuse. If Syria commits human rights abuses and resists U.S. economic or military domination, and if Bahrain commits human rights abuses but lets the U.S. Navy dock a fleet of ships in its harbor, the response should be the same. In fact, the fleets of ships should come home from other countries' harbors, which would make the even-handedness easier. The dictators overthrown in recent years by nonviolence in Egypt, Yemen, and Tunisia had, but should not have had, U.S. support. The same goes for the dictator overthrown violently in Libya and the one threatened in Syria, as well as the one overthrown in Iraq. These were all people with whom the U.S. government was happy to work when it seemed to be in U.S. interests. The United States should stop arming, funding, or supporting in any way governments that commit human rights abuses, including the governments of Israel and Egypt. And, of course, the United States should not commit human rights abuses itself.

Third, individuals, groups, and governments should support nonviolent resistance to tyranny and abuse, except when association with them will so discredit those supported as to be counterproductive. Nonviolent victories over tyrannical governments tend to be more frequent and longer lasting than violent ones, and those trends are increasing. (I recommend Erica Chenoweth's and Maria J. Stephan's *Why Civil Resistance Works: The Strategic Logic of Nonviolent Conflict*.)

Fourth, a government that goes to war against its own people or another country should be shamed, ostracized, prosecuted, sanctioned (in a manner imposing pressure on the government, not suffering on its people), reasoned with, and moved in a peaceful direction. Conversely, governments that do not commit genocide or war should be rewarded.

Fifth, the nations of the world should establish an international police force independent of the interests of any nation engaged in military expansionism or the stationing of troops and weapons in foreign nations around the globe. Such a police force needs to have the sole aim of defending human rights and to be understood to have only that aim. It also needs to use the tools of policing, not the tools of war. Bombing Rwanda wouldn't have done anyone any good. Police on the ground could have. Bombing Kosovo resulted in increased killing on the ground, not cessation of war.

Of course we should prevent and oppose genocide. But using war to stop genocide is like having sex for virginity. War and genocide are twins. The distinction between them is often that wars are made by our country and genocides by others". Historian Peter Kuznick asks his classes how many people the United States killed in Vietnam. Students often guess no more than 50,000. Then he tells them that former Secretary of "Defense" Robert McNamara was in his classroom and acknowledged that it was 3.8 million. That was the conclusion of a 2008 study by Harvard Medical School and the Institute for Health Metrics and Evaluation at the University of Washington. Nick Turse's *Kill Anything That Moves* suggests that the real number is higher.

Kuznick then asks his students how many people Hitler killed in concentration camps, and they all know the answer to be 6 million Jews (and millions more including all victims). He asks what they would think if Germans failed to know the number and to feel historical guilt over it. The contrast in Germany is in fact striking with how U.S. students think—if they think at all—about U.S. killing in the Philippines, Vietnam, Cambodia, Laos, Iraq, or—indeed—in World War II.

A War on Genocide?

While the genocide of several million in Germany was as horrific as anything imaginable, the war took 50 to 70 million lives total. Some 3 million Japanese died, including hundreds of thousands in air raids prior to the two nuclear bombs that killed some 225,000. Germany killed more Soviet troops than it killed prisoners. The allies killed more Germans than Germany did. They may have done so for a higher purpose, but not without a certain murderous glee on the part of some as well. Prior to U.S.

entry into the war, Harry Truman stood up in the Senate and said that the United States should help either the Germans or the Russians, whoever was losing, so that more people would die.

"Kill anything that moves" was an order that showed up, in various wording, in Iraq as in Vietnam. But various anti-personnel weapons, such as cluster bombs, were used in Vietnam specifically to maim and horribly injure rather than to kill, and some of those same weapons are still used by the United States. (See Turse, p. 77.) War can't fix anything worse than war because there isn't anything worse than war.

The answer to "what would you do if one country attacked another?" should be the same as the answer to "what would you do if a country committed genocide?" Pundits express their greatest outrage at a tyrant who is "killing his own people." In fact, killing someone else's people is evil too. It is even evil when NATO does it.

Should we go to war or sit by? Those are not the only choices. What would I do, I've been asked more than once, rather than killing people with drones? I've always replied: *I'd refrain from killing people with drones.* I'd also treat criminal suspects as criminal suspects and work to see them prosecuted for their crimes.

The Case of Libya

I think a bit of detail on a couple of specific cases, Libya and Syria, is justified here by the alarming tendency of many who claim they oppose war to make exceptions for particular wars, including these—one a recent war, the other a threatened war at the time of this writing. First, Libya.

The humanitarian argument for the 2011 NATO bombing of Libya is that it prevented a massacre or it improved a nation by overthrowing a bad government. Much of the weaponry on both sides of the war was U.S. made. The Hitler of the moment had enjoyed U.S. support off-and-on in the past. But taking the moment for what it was, regardless of what might have been done better in the past to avoid it, the case is still not a strong one.

The White House claimed that Gaddafi had threated to massacre the people of Benghazi with "no mercy," but the *New York Times* reported that Gaddafi's threat was directed at rebel fighters, not civilians, and that Gaddafi promised amnesty for those "who throw their weapons away." Gaddafi also offered to allow rebel fighters to escape to Egypt if they preferred not to fight to the death. Yet President Obama warned of imminent genocide.

The above report of what Gaddafi really threatened fits with his past behavior. There were other opportunities for massacres had he wished to commit massacres, in Zawiya, Misurata, or Ajdabiya. He did not do so. After extensive fighting in Misurata, a report by Human Rights Watch made clear that Gaddafi had targeted fighters, not civilians. Of 400,000 people in Misurata, 257 died in two months of fighting. Out of 949 wounded, less than 3 percent were women.

More likely than genocide was defeat for the rebels, the same rebels who warned Western media of the looming genocide, the same rebels who the *New York Times* said "feel no loyalty to the truth in shaping their propaganda" and who were "making vastly inflated claims of [Gaddafi's] barbaric behavior." The result of NATO joining the war was probably more killing, not less. It certainly extended a war that looked likely to end soon with a victory for Gaddafi.

Alan Kuperman pointed out in the *Boston Globe* that "Obama embraced the noble principle of the responsibility to protect— which some quickly dubbed the Obama Doctrine—calling for intervention when possible to prevent genocide. Libya reveals how this approach, implemented reflexively, may backfire by encouraging rebels to provoke and exaggerate atrocities, to entice intervention that ultimately perpetuates civil war and humanitarian suffering."

But what of the overthrow of Gaddafi? That was accomplished whether or not a massacre was prevented. True. And it is too early to say what the full results are. But we do know this: strength was given to the idea that it is acceptable for a group of governments to violently overthrow another. Violent overthrows almost always leave behind instability and resentment. Violence spilled over into Mali and other nations in the region. Rebels with no interest in democracy or civil rights were armed and empowered, with possible repercussions in Syria, for a U.S. ambassador killed in Benghazi, and in future blowback. And a lesson was taught to other nations' rulers: if you disarm (as Libya, like Iraq, had given up its nuclear and chemical weapons programs) you may be attacked.

In other dubious precedents, the war was fought in opposition to the will of the U.S. Congress and the United Nations. Overthrowing governments may be popular, but it isn't actually legal. So, other justifications had to be invented. The U.S Department of Justice submitted to Congress a written defense claiming the war served the U.S. national interest in regional stability and in maintaining the credibility of the United Nations. But are Libya and the United States in the same region? What region is that, *earth*? And isn't a revolution the opposite of stability?

The credibility of the United Nations is an unusual concern, coming from a government that invaded Iraq in 2003 despite UN opposition and for the express purpose (among others) of proving the UN irrelevant. The same government, within weeks of making this case to Congress, refused to allow the UN special rapporteur to visit a U.S. prisoner named Bradley Manning (now named Chelsea Manning) to verify that she was not being tortured. The same government authorized the CIA to violate the UN arms embargo in Libya, violated the UN ban on "a foreign occupation force of any form" in Libya, and proceeded without hesitation from actions in Benghazi authorized by the UN to actions around the country aimed at "regime change."

Popular "progressive" U.S. radio host Ed Schultz argued, with vicious hatred in every word he spat out on the subject, that bombing Libya was justified by the need for vengeance against that Satan on earth, that beast arisen suddenly from the grave of Adolph Hitler, that monster beyond all description: Muammar Gaddafi.

Popular U.S. commentator Juan Cole supported the very same war as an act of humanitarian generosity. Many people in NATO countries are motivated by humanitarian concern; that's why wars are sold as acts of philanthropy. But the U.S. government does not typically intervene in other nations in order to benefit humanity. And to be accurate, the United States is not capable of intervening anywhere, because it is already intervened everywhere; what we call intervention is better called violently switching sides.

The United States was in the business of supplying weapons to Gaddafi up until the moment it got into the business of supplying weapons to his opponents. In 2009, Britain, France and other European states sold Libya over $470m-worth of weapons. The United States can no more intervene in Yemen or Bahrain or Saudi Arabia than in Libya. The U.S. government is arming those dictatorships. In fact, to win the support of Saudi Arabia for its "intervention" in Libya, the U.S. gave its approval for Saudi Arabia to send troops into Bahrain to attack civilians, a policy that U.S. Secretary of State Hillary Clinton publicly defended.

The "humanitarian intervention" in Libya, meanwhile, whatever civilians it may have begun by protecting, immediately killed other civilians with its bombs and immediately shifted from its defensive justification to attacking retreating troops and participating in a civil war.

Washington imported a leader for the people's rebellion in Libya who had spent the previous 20 years living with no known source of income a couple of miles from the CIA's headquarters in Virginia. Another man lives even closer to CIA headquarters: former U.S. Vice President Dick Cheney. He expressed great concern in a speech in 1999 that foreign governments were controlling oil. "Oil remains fundamentally a government business," he said. "While many regions of the world offer great oil opportunities, the Middle East, with two thirds of the world's oil and the lowest cost, is still where the prize ultimately lies." Former supreme allied commander Europe of NATO, from 1997 to 2000, Wesley Clark claims that in 2001, a general in the Pentagon showed him a piece of paper and said:

> *I just got this memo today or yesterday from the office of the secretary of defense upstairs. It's a, it's a five-year plan. We're going to take down seven countries in five years. We're going to start with Iraq, then Syria, Lebanon, then Libya, Somalia, Sudan, we're going to come back and get Iran in five years.*

That agenda fit perfectly with the plans of Washington insiders, such as those who famously spelled out their intentions in the reports of the think tank called the Project for the New American Century. The fierce Iraqi and Afghan resistance didn't fit in the plan at all. Neither did the nonviolent revolutions in Tunisia and Egypt. But taking over Libya still made perfect sense in the neoconservative worldview. And it made sense in explaining war games used by Britain and France to simulate the invasion of a similar country.

The Libyan government controlled more of its oil than any other nation on earth, and it was the type of oil that Europe finds easiest to refine. Libya also controlled its own finances, leading American author Ellen Brown to point out an interesting fact about those seven countries named by Clark:

"What do these seven countries have in common? In the context of banking, one that sticks out is that none of them is listed among the 56 member banks of the Bank for International Settlements (BIS). That evidently puts them outside the long regulatory arm of the central bankers' central bank in Switzerland. The most renegade of the lot could be Libya and Iraq, the two that have actually been attacked. Kenneth Schortgen Jr., writing on Examiner.com, noted that '[s]ix months before the US moved into Iraq to take down Saddam Hussein, the oil nation had made the move to accept euros instead of dollars for oil, and this became a threat to the global dominance of the dollar as the reserve currency, and its dominion as the petrodollar.' According to a Russian article titled 'Bombing of Libya – Punishment for Gaddafi for His Attempt to Refuse US Dollar', Gaddafi made a similarly bold move: he initiated a movement to refuse the dollar and the euro, and called on Arab and African nations to use a new currency instead, the gold dinar.

"Gaddafi suggested establishing a united African continent, with its 200 million people using this single currency. During the past year, the idea was approved by many Arab countries and most African countries. The only opponents were the Republic of South Africa and the head of the League of Arab States. The initiative was viewed negatively by the U.S. and the European Union, with French President Nicolas Sarkozy calling Libya a threat to the financial security of mankind; but Gaddafi was not swayed and continued his push for the creation of a united Africa."

The Case of Syria

Syria, like Libya, was on the list cited by Clark, and on a similar list attributed to Dick Cheney by former British Prime Minister Tony Blair in his memoirs. U.S. officials, including Senator John McCain, have for years openly expressed a desire to overthrow the government of Syria because it is allied with the government of Iran which they believe must also be overthrown. Iran's 2013 elections didn't seem to alter that imperative.

As I was writing this, the U.S. government was promoting U.S. war-making in Syria on the grounds that the Syrian government had used chemical weapons. No solid evidence for this claim had yet been offered. Below are 12 reasons why this latest excuse for war is no good *even if true.*

1. War is not made legal by such an excuse. It can't be found in the Kellogg-Briand Pact, the United Nations Charter, or the U.S. Constitution. It can, however, be found in U.S. war propaganda of the 2002 vintage. (Who says our government doesn't promote recycling?)

2. The United States itself possesses and uses chemical and other internationally condemned weapons, including white phosphorus, napalm, cluster bombs, and depleted uranium. Whether you praise these actions, avoid thinking about them, or join me in

condemning them, they are not a legal or moral justification for any foreign nation to bomb us, or to bomb some other nation where the U.S. military is operating. Killing people to prevent their being killed with the wrong kind of weapons is a policy that must come out of some sort of sickness. Call it Pre-Traumatic Stress Disorder.

3. An expanded war in Syria could become regional or global with uncontrollable consequences. Syria, Lebanon, Iran, Russia, China, the United States, the Gulf states, the NATO states ... does this sound like the sort of conflict we want? Does it sound like a conflict anyone will survive? Why in the world risk such a thing?

4. Just creating a "no fly zone" would involve bombing urban areas and unavoidably killing large numbers of people. This happened in Libya and we looked away. But it would happen on a much larger scale in Syria, given the locations of the sites to be bombed. Creating a "no fly zone" is not a matter of making an announcement, but of dropping bombs on anti-aircraft weaponry.

5. Both sides in Syria have used horrible weapons and committed horrible atrocities. Surely even those who imagine people should be killed to prevent their being killed with different weapons can see the insanity of arming both sides to protect each other side. Why is it not, then, just as insane to arm one side in a conflict that involves similar abuses by both?

6. With the United States on the side of the opposition in Syria, the United States will be blamed for the opposition's crimes. Most

people in Western Asia hate al Qaeda and other terrorists. They are also coming to hate the United States and its drones, missiles, bases, night raids, lies, and hypocrisy. Imagine the levels of hatred that will be reached if al Qaeda and the United States team up to overthrow the government of Syria and create an Iraq-like hell in its place.

7. An unpopular rebellion put into power by outside force does not usually result in a stable government. In fact there is not yet on record a case of U.S. humanitarian war clearly benefitting humanity or of nation-building actually building a nation. Why would Syria, which looks even less auspicious than most potential targets, be the exception to the rule?

8. This opposition is not interested in creating a democracy, or—for that matter—in taking instructions from the U.S. government. On the contrary, blowback from these allies is likely. Just as we should have learned the lesson of lies about weapons by now, our government should have learned the lesson of arming the enemy of the enemy long before this moment.

9. The precedent of another lawless act by the United States, whether arming proxies or engaging directly, sets a dangerous example to the world and to those in Washington and in Israel for whom Iran is next on the list.

10. A strong majority of Americans, despite all the media's efforts thus far, opposes arming the rebels or engaging directly. Instead, a plurality supports providing humanitarian aid. And many (most?)

Syrians, regardless of the strength of their criticism for the current government, oppose foreign interference and violence. Many of the rebels are, in fact, foreign fighters. We might better spread democracy by example than by bomb.

11. There are nonviolent pro-democracy movements in Bahrain and Turkey and elsewhere, and in Syria itself, and our government doesn't lift a finger in support.

12. Establishing that the government of Syria has done horrible things or that the people of Syria are suffering, doesn't make a case for taking actions likely to make matters worse. There is a major crisis with refugees fleeing Syria in large numbers, but there are as many or more Iraqi refugees still unable to return to their homes. Lashing out at another Hitler might satisfy a certain urge, but it will not benefit the people of Syria. The people of Syria are just as valuable as the people of the United States. There is no reason Americans shouldn't risk their lives for Syrians. But Americans arming Syrians or bombing Syrians in an action likely to exacerbate the crisis does no one any good at all. We should be encouraging de-escalation and dialogue, disarmament of both sides, the departure of foreign fighters, the return of refugees, the provision of humanitarian aid, the prosecution of war crimes, reconciliation among groups, and the holding of free elections.

Nobel Peace Laureate Mairead Maguire visited Syria and discussed the state of affairs there on my radio show. She wrote in *the Guardian* that, "while there is a legitimate and long-overdue movement for peace and non-violent reform in Syria, the worst acts of violence are being perpetrated by outside groups. Extremist groups from around the world have converged upon Syria, bent on turning this conflict into one of ideological hatred. ... International peacekeepers, as well as experts and civilians inside Syria, are nearly unanimous in their view that United States involvement would only worsen this conflict."

You Can't Use War to End War

In 1928, the major nations of the world signed the Kellogg-Briand Pact, also known as the Peace Pact or the Pact of Paris, which renounced war and committed nations to resolving international disputes by peaceful means alone. Abolitionists hoped to develop a system of international law, arbitration, and prosecution, and to see wars prevented through diplomacy, targeted sanctions, and other nonviolent pressures. Many believed that proposals to enforce a ban on war through the use of war-making would be self-defeating. In 1931, Senator William Borah remarked:

Much has been said, and will continue to be said, for the doctrine of force dies hard, about implementing the peace pact. It is said that we must put teeth into it—an apt word revealing again that theory of peace which is based upon tearing, maiming, destroying, murdering. Many have inquired of me: What is meant by implementing the peace pact? I will seek to make it plain. What they mean is to change the peace pact into a military pact. They would transform it into another peace scheme based upon force, and force is another name for war. By putting teeth into it, they mean an agreement to employ armies and navies

> *wherever the fertile mind of some ambitious schemer can*
> *find an aggressor ... I have no language to express my horror*
> *of this proposal to build peace treaties, or peace schemes,*
> *upon the doctrine of force.*

Because World War II proceeded to occur, the common wisdom is that Borah was wrong, that the pact needed teeth. Thus the U.N. Charter includes provisions for the use of war to combat war. But during the Twenties and Thirties the U.S. and other governments weren't just signing a peace treaty. They were also buying more and more weaponry, failing to develop an adequate system of international law, and encouraging dangerous trends in places like Germany, Italy, and Japan. Following the war, making use of the pact, the victors prosecuted the losers for the crime of war-making. This was a first in world history. Judged by the absence of World War III (also probably attributable to other causes, including the existence of nuclear weapons) those first prosecutions were remarkably successful.

Judged by the first half-century of the United Nations and NATO, schemes for ending war through force remain deeply flawed. The U.N. Charter permits wars that are either defensive or U.N. authorized, so the U.S. has described attacking unarmed impoverished nations halfway around the globe as defensive and U.N.-approved whether or not that has actually been the case. NATO nations' agreement to come to each other's aid has been transformed into collective assaults on distant lands. The tool of force, as Borah understood, will be used according to the desires of whoever has the most force.

Of course, many involved will mean well as they grow outraged at dictators their government drops its support for and begins opposing, and as they demand to know whether we should do something or nothing in the face of attacks on innocents—as if the only choices are war and sitting on our hands. The answer, of course, is that we should do many somethings. But one of them is not war.

The Wrong Kind of War Opposition

There are ways to oppose war that are less than ideal, because they're based on falsehoods, are limited by their nature to opposing only some wars, and don't generate a sufficient level of passion and activism. This is true even once we get beyond opposing only wars by non-Western states. There are ways in which to oppose particular U.S. wars that don't necessarily advance the cause of abolition.

A majority of Americans, in several recent polls, believes the 2003-2011 war on Iraq hurt the United States but benefitted Iraq. A plurality of Americans believes, not only that Iraqis *should* be grateful, but that Iraqis *are* in fact grateful. Many Americans who favored ending the war for years while it continued, favored ending an act of philanthropy. Having heard mainly about U.S. troops and U.S. budgets from the U.S. media, and even from U.S. peace groups, these people had no idea that their government had inflicted on Iraq one of the most damaging attacks ever suffered by any nation.

Now, I'm not eager to refuse anyone's war opposition, and I would not want to take it away. But I don't have to do that in order to try to augment it. The Iraq war did hurt the United States. It did cost the United States. But it hurt Iraqis on a much larger scale. This matters not because we should feel the appropriate level of guilt or inferiority, but because opposing wars for limited reasons results in limited war opposition. If the Iraq war cost too much, maybe the Libya war was affordably priced. If too many U.S. soldiers died in Iraq, maybe drone strikes solve that problem. Opposition to the costs of war for the aggressor may be strong, but is it likely to build as dedicated a movement as opposition to those costs combined with righteous opposition to mass murder?

Congressman Walter Jones cheered the 2003 invasion of Iraq, and when France opposed it, he insisted on renaming french fries, freedom fries. But the suffering of U.S. troops changed his mind. Many were from his district. He saw what they went through, what their families went through. It was enough. But he didn't get to know Iraqis. He didn't act on their behalf.

When President Obama began talking about war in Syria, Congressman Jones introduced a resolution essentially restating the Constitution and the War Powers Act, by requiring that Congress give approval before the launching of any war. The resolution got many points right (or close to it):

> *Whereas the Constitution's makers entrusted decisions to initiate offensive warfare not in self-defense exclusively to Congress in article I, section 8, clause 11;*

Whereas the Constitution's makers knew that the Executive Branch would be prone to manufacture danger and to deceive Congress and the United States people to justify gratuitous wars to aggrandize executive power;

Whereas chronic wars are irreconcilable with liberty, a separation of powers, and the rule of law;

Whereas the entry of the United States Armed Forces into the ongoing war in Syria to overthrow President Bashar al-Assad would make the United States less safe by awakening new enemies;

Whereas humanitarian wars are a contradiction in terms and characteristically lead to semi-anarchy and chaos, as in Somalia and Libya;

Whereas if victorious, the hydra-headed Syrian insurgency would suppress the Christian population or other minorities as has been similarly witnessed in Iraq with its Shiite-dominated government; and

Whereas United States military aid to the Syrian insurgents risks blowback indistinguishable from the military assistance provided to the splintered Afghan mujahideen in Afghanistan to oppose the Soviet Union and culminated in the 9/11 abominations.

But the following gratuitous piece of bigotry marred the

resolution and played right into the hands of the "humanitarian" warriors:

> *Whereas the fate of Syria is irrelevant to the security and welfare of the United States and its citizens and is not worth risking the life of a single member of the United States Armed Forces.*

The fate of an entire nation of some 20 million people is not worth a single person, if the 20 million are Syrians and the 1 is from the United States? Why would that be? Of course, the fate of Syria is relevant to the rest of the world—see the paragraph above regarding blowback. Jones' unnecessary nationalism will convince many of his ignorance. He plays right into the idea that a war on Syria would benefit Syrians but cost the United States. He encourages the idea that no one should risk their life for others, unless those others are from the same little tribe. Our world won't survive the coming environmental crises with that mindset. Jones is aware that Syria would suffer—see the paragraphs above. He should say so. The fact that our wars have no upside, that they hurt both us and their supposed beneficiaries, that they make us less safe while slaughtering human beings, is a stronger case. And it's a case against all war-making, not just some of it.

The Costs of War

The costs of war are mostly on the other side. U.S. deaths in Iraq totaled 0.3 percent of the deaths in that war (See WarIsACrime.org/Iraq). But the costs back home are also much more extensive than is commonly recognized. We hear about the deaths more than the far more numerous injuries. We hear about the visible injuries more than the far more numerous invisible injuries: the brain injuries and the mental pain and anguish. We don't hear enough about the suicides, or the impact on families and friends.

The financial cost of wars is presented as enormous, and it is. But it is dwarfed by routine non-war spending on war preparations—spending that, according to the National Priorities Project, combined with war spending, accounts for 57 percent of federal discretionary spending in the President's proposed budget for 2014. And all of that spending is falsely presented to us as at least having the silver lining of economic benefit. In fact, however, according to repeated studies by the University of Massachusetts - Amherst, military spending produces fewer and worse-paying jobs than just about any other kind of spending, including education, infrastructure, green energy, etc. In fact, military spending is worse for the economy than tax cuts for working people—or, in other words, worse than nothing. It's an economic drain presented as a "Job Creator," just like the fine folks who make up the Forbes 400 (See PERI.UMass.edu).

Ironically, while "freedom" is often cited as a reason for fighting a war, our wars have long been used as justifications to seriously curtail our actual freedoms. Compare the fourth, fifth, and first amendments to the U.S. Constitution with common U.S. practice now and 15 years ago if you think I'm kidding. During the "global war on terror," the U.S. government has established serious restrictions on public demonstrations, massive surveillance programs in blatant violation of the Fourth Amendment, the open practice of indefinite imprisonment without charge or trial, an ongoing program of assassinations by secret presidential orders, and immunity for those who commit the crime of torture on behalf of the U.S. government. Some large non-governmental organizations do a terrific job of addressing these symptoms but intentionally avoid addressing the disease of war-making and war preparation.

The culture of war, the weapons of war, and the profit-making functions of war are transferred into an ever more militarized domestic police force, and ever more warlike immigration control. But police viewing the public as an enemy rather than an employer doesn't make us safer. It puts our immediate safety and our hopes for representative government at risk.

Wartime secrecy takes government away from the people and characterizes whistleblowers who try to inform us about what is being done, in our names, with our money, as national enemies. We're taught to hate those who respect us and to defer to those who hold us in contempt. As I was writing this, a young whistleblower named Bradley Manning (now named Chelsea Manning) was put on trial for revealing war crimes. She was charged with "aiding the enemy" and with violating the World War I-era Espionage Act. No evidence was presented that she'd aided any enemy or attempted to aid any enemy, and she was acquitted on the charge of "aiding the enemy." Yet she was found guilty of "espionage," purely for fulfilling her legal and moral responsibility to expose government wrong-doing. At the same time, another young whistleblower, Edward Snowden, fled the country in fear for his life. And numerous reporters said that sources within the government were refusing any longer to speak to them. The federal government has established an "Insider Threat Program," encouraging government employees to snitch on any employees they suspect of becoming whistleblowers or spies.

Our culture, our morality, our sense of decency: these can be casualties of war even when the war is thousands of miles off-shore.

Our natural environment is a primary victim as well, these wars over fossil fuels being themselves leading consumers of fossil fuels, and poisoners of earth, air, and water in a wide variety of ways. The acceptability of war in our culture can be gauged by the large environmental groups' unwillingness thus far to take on one of the most destructive forces in existence: the war machine. I asked James Marriott, co-author of *The Oil Road,* whether he thought fossil fuel use contributed more to militarism or militarism more to fossil fuel use. He replied, "You're not going to get rid of one without the other" (only a mild exaggeration, I think).

As we put our resources and energy into war we lose out in other areas: education, parks, vacations, retirements. We have the best military and the best prisons, but trail far behind in everything from schools to healthcare to internet and phone systems.

In 2011, I helped organize a conference called "The Military Industrial Complex at 50" that looked at many of the types of damage the military industrial complex does (See DavidSwanson. org/mic50). The occasion was the half-century mark since President Eisenhower found the nerve in his farewell speech to articulate one of the most prescient, potentially valuable, and tragically as yet unheeded warnings of human history:

> *In the councils of government, we must guard against the acquisition of unwarranted influence, whether sought or unsought, by the military-industrial complex. The potential for the disastrous rise of misplaced power exists and will persist. We must never let the weight of this combination endanger our liberties or democratic processes. We should take nothing for granted. Only an alert and knowledgeable citizenry can compel the proper meshing of the huge industrial and military machinery of defense with our peaceful methods and goals, so that security and liberty may prosper together.*

Another World Is Possible

A world *without* war could be a world *with* many things we want and many things we don't dare dream of. This book's cover is celebratory because war's abolition would mean the end of a barbaric horror, but also because of what could follow. Peace and freedom from fear are far more liberating than bombs. That liberation could mean a birth for culture, for art, for science, for prosperity. We could begin by treating top-quality education from pre-school to college as a human right, not to mention housing, healthcare, vacation, and retirement. We could raise lifespans, happiness, intelligence, political participation, and prospects for a sustainable future.

We don't need war in order to maintain our lifestyle. We need to shift to solar, wind, and other renewables if we are going to survive.

Doing so has many advantages. For one thing, a given country will be unlikely to hoard more than its fair share of sunshine. There's plenty to go around, and it's best used near where it's gathered. We may want to improve our lifestyle in some ways, growing more local food, developing local economies, reversing the unequal concentration of wealth that I called medieval until a professor pointed out that medieval economies were more equitable than ours. Americans need not suffer in order to treat resources more equitably and with careful stewardship.

Public support for war, and participation in the military, draw in part on qualities often romanticized about war and warriors: excitement, sacrifice, loyalty, bravery, and camaraderie. These can indeed be found in war, but not exclusively in war. Examples of all these qualities, plus compassion, empathy, and respect are found not only in war, but also in the work of humanitarians, activists, and healers. A world without war need not lose excitement or bravery. Nonviolent activism will fill that gap, as will proper responses to the forest fires and floods that lie in our future as our climate changes. We need these variations on glory and adventure if we are to survive. As a side benefit they render any argument for the positive aspects of war-making moot. It's been a long time since William James sought an alternative for all the positive aspects of war, the courage, solidarity, sacrifice, etc. It's also been a long time since Mohandas Gandhi found one.

Of course, environmental apocalypse is not the only kind of super-catastrophe that threatens. As nuclear weaponry proliferates, as drone technology proliferates, and as the hunting of humans becomes routine, we also risk nuclear and other war-related disaster. Ending war is not just a path toward utopia; it's also the way to survival. But, as Eisenhower warned, we cannot eliminate war without eliminating war preparations. And we cannot eliminate war preparations without eliminating the idea that a good war may come along some day. To do that, it will certainly help if we eliminate, or at least weaken, the idea that we've seen good wars in the past.

"There Never Was A Good War or a Bad Peace" or How to Be Against Both Hitler and War

Benjamin Franklin, who said that bit inside the quotation marks, lived before Hitler and so may not be qualified—in the minds of many—to speak on the matter. But World War II happened in a very different world from today's, didn't need to happen, and could have been dealt with differently when it did happen. It also happened differently from how we are usually taught. For one thing, the U.S. government was eager to enter the war, and to a great extent did enter the war, in both the Atlantic and the Pacific, prior to Pearl Harbor.

Pre-WWII Germany might have looked very different without the harsh settlement that followed World War I which punished an entire people rather than the war makers, and without the significant monetary support provided for decades past and ongoing through World War II by U.S. corporations like GM, Ford, IBM, and ITT (see *Wall Street and the Rise of Hitler* by Anthony Sutton).

(Let me insert a parenthetical remark here that I hope many will find quite silly, but that I know others will need to hear. We are talking about World War II, and I've just criticized someone other than Hitler—namely U.S. corporations—so let me hasten to point out that Hitler still gets to be responsible for every hideous crime he committed. Blame is more like sunshine than like fossil fuels; we can give some to Henry Ford for his support of Hitler without taking the slightest bit away from Adolph Hitler himself and without comparing or equating the two.)

Nonviolent resistance to the Nazis in Denmark, Holland, and Norway, as well as the successful protests in Berlin by the non-Jewish wives of imprisoned Jewish husbands suggested a potential that was never fully realized—not even close. The notion that Germany could have maintained a lasting occupation of the rest of Europe and the Soviet Union, and proceeded to attack in the Americas, is extremely unlikely, even given the 1940s' relatively limited knowledge of nonviolent activism. Militarily, Germany was primarily defeated by the Soviet Union, its other enemies playing relatively minor parts.

The important point is not that massive, organized nonviolence should have been used against the Nazis in the 1940s. It wasn't, and many people would have had to see the world very differently in order for that to have happened. Rather the point is that tools of nonviolence are much more widely understood today and can be, and typically will be, used against rising tyrants. We should not imagine returning to an age in which that wasn't so, even if doing so helps to justify outrageous levels of military spending!

We should, rather, strengthen our efforts to nonviolently resist the growth of tyrannical powers before they reach a crisis point, and to simultaneously resist efforts to lay the ground work for future wars against them.

Prior to the attack on Pearl Harbor, which was not then part of the United States, President Franklin Roosevelt had tried lying to the American people about U.S. ships including the *Greer* and the *Kearny,* which had been helping British planes track German submarines, but which Roosevelt pretended had been wrongly attacked. Roosevelt also tried to create support for entering the war by lying that he had in his possession a secret Nazi map planning the conquest of South America, as well as a secret Nazi plan for replacing all religions with Nazism. However, the people of the United States rejected the idea of going into another war until the Japanese attack on Pearl Harbor, by which point Roosevelt had already instituted the draft, activated the National Guard, created and begun using a huge Navy in two oceans, traded old destroyers to England in exchange for the lease of its bases in the Caribbean and Bermuda, and secretly ordered the creation of a list of every Japanese and Japanese-American person in the United States.

When President Roosevelt visited Pearl Harbor seven years before the Japanese attack, the Japanese military (which, just like Hitler or anyone else in the world, gets full blame for all of its inexcusable crimes) expressed apprehension. In March 1935, Roosevelt bestowed Wake Island on the U.S. Navy and gave Pan Am Airways a permit to build runways on Wake Island, Midway Island, and Guam. Japanese military commanders announced that they were disturbed and viewed these runways as a threat. So did peace activists in the United States.

In November 1940, Roosevelt loaned China $100m for war with Japan, and after consulting with the British, U.S. Secretary of the Treasury Henry Morgenthau made plans to send the Chinese bombers with U.S. crews to use in bombing Tokyo and other Japanese cities.

For years prior to the attack on Pearl Harbor, the U.S. Navy worked on plans for war with Japan, the March 8, 1939, version of which described "an offensive war of long duration" that would destroy the military and disrupt the economic life of Japan. In January 1941, the *Japan Advertiser* expressed its outrage over Pearl Harbor in an editorial, and the U.S. ambassador to Japan wrote in his diary: "There is a lot of talk around town to the effect that the Japanese, in case of a break with the United States, are planning to go all out in a surprise mass attack on Pearl Harbor. Of course I informed my government."

On May 24, 1941, the *New York Times* reported on U.S. training of the Chinese air force, and the provision of "numerous fighting and bombing planes" to China by the United States. "Bombing of Japanese Cities is Expected" read the subheadline.

On July 24, 1941, President Roosevelt remarked, "If we cut the oil off, [the Japanese] probably would have gone down to the Dutch East Indies a year ago, and you would have had a war. It was very essential from our own selfish point of view of defense to prevent a war from starting in the South Pacific. So our foreign policy was trying to stop a war from breaking out there." Reporters noticed that Roosevelt said "was" rather than "is." The next day, Roosevelt issued an executive order freezing Japanese assets. The United States and Britain cut off oil and scrap metal to Japan. Radhabinod Pal, an Indian jurist who served on the war crimes tribunal in Tokyo after the war, called the embargoes a "clear and potent threat to Japan's very existence," and concluded the United States had provoked Japan.

The U.S. government is imposing what it proudly calls "crippling sanctions" on Iran as I write.

On November 15, 1941, Army Chief of Staff George Marshall briefed the media on something we do not remember as "the Marshall Plan." In fact we don't remember it at all. "We are preparing an offensive war against Japan," Marshall said, asking the journalists to keep it a secret.

Ten days later Secretary of War Henry Stimson wrote in his diary that he'd met in the Oval Office with Marshall, President Roosevelt, Secretary of the Navy Frank Knox, Admiral Harold Stark, and Secretary of State Cordell Hull. Roosevelt had told them the Japanese were likely to attack soon, possibly next Monday. It has been well documented that the United States had broken the Japanese' codes and that Roosevelt had access to them.

What did not bring the United States into the war or keep it going was a desire to save Jews from persecution. For years Roosevelt blocked legislation that would have allowed Jewish refugees from

Germany into the United States. The notion of a war to save the Jews is found on none of the war propaganda posters and essentially arose after the war was over, just as the idea of the "good war" took hold decades later as a comparison to the Vietnam War.

"Disturbed in 1942," wrote Lawrence S. Wittner, "by rumors of Nazi extermination plans, Jessie Wallace Hughan, an educator, a politician, and a founder of the War Resisters League, worried that such a policy, which appeared 'natural, from their pathological point of view,' might be carried out if World War II continued. 'It seems that the only way to save thousands and perhaps millions of European Jews from destruction,' she wrote, 'would be for our government to broadcast the promise' of an 'armistice on condition that the European minorities are not molested any further. ... It would be very terrible if six months from now we should find that this threat has literally come to pass without our making even a gesture to prevent it.' When her predictions were fulfilled only too well by 1943, she wrote to the State Department and the *New York Times,* decrying the fact that 'two million [Jews] have already died' and that 'two million more will be killed by the end of the war.' Once again she pleaded for the cessation of hostilities, arguing that German military defeats would in turn exact reprisals upon the Jewish scapegoat. 'Victory will not save them,' she insisted, 'for dead men cannot be liberated.'"

In the end some prisoners were rescued, but many more had been killed. Not only did the war not prevent the genocide, but the war itself was worse. The war established that civilians were fair game for mass slaughter and slaughtered them by the tens of millions. Attempts to shock and awe through mass slaughter failed. Fire-bombing cities served no higher purpose. Dropping one, and then a second, nuclear bomb was in no way justified as a way to end a war that was already ending. German and Japanese imperialism were halted, but the U.S. global empire of bases and wars was born—bad news for the Middle East, Latin America, Korea, Vietnam, Cambodia, Laos, and elsewhere. The Nazi ideology was not defeated by violence. Many Nazi scientists were brought over to work for the Pentagon, the results of their influence apparent.

But much of what we think of as particularly Nazi evils (eugenics, human experimentation, etc.) could be found in the United States as well, before, during, and after the war. A recent book called *Against Their Will: The Secret History of Medical Experimentation on Children in Cold War America* collects much of what is known. Eugenics was taught in hundreds of medical schools in the United States by the 1920s and by one estimate in three-quarters of U.S. colleges by the mid 1930s. Non-consensual experimentation on institutionalized children and adults was common in the United States before, during, and especially after the U.S. and its allies prosecuted Nazis for the practice in 1947, sentencing many to prison and seven to be hanged. The tribunal created the Nuremberg Code, standards for medical practice that were immediately ignored back home. American doctors considered it "a good code for barbarians." Thus, we had the Tuskegee syphilis study, and the experimentation at the Jewish Chronic Disease Hospital in Brooklyn, the Willowbrook State School on Staten Island, Holmesburg Prison in Philadelphia, and so many others, including U.S. experiments on Guatemalans during the Nuremberg proceedings. Also during the Nuremberg trial, children at the Pennhurst school in southeastern Pennsylvania were given hepatitis-laced feces to eat. Human experimentation increased in the decades that followed. As each story has leaked out we've seen it as an aberration. *Against Their Will* suggests otherwise. As I write, there are protests of recent forced sterilizations of women in California prisons.

The point is not to compare the relative levels of evilness of individuals or people. The Nazis' concentration camps are very hard to match in that regard. The point is that no side in a war is *good*, and evil behavior is no justification for war. American Curtis LeMay, who oversaw the fire bombing of Japanese cities, killing hundreds of thousands of civilians, said that if the other side had won he'd have been prosecuted as a war criminal. That scenario wouldn't have rendered the disgusting war crimes of the Japanese or the Germans acceptable or praiseworthy. But it would have led to the world giving them less thought, or at least less exclusive thought. Instead, the crimes of the allies would be the focus, or at least one focus, of outrage.

You need not think that U.S. entry into World War II was a bad idea in order to oppose all future wars. You can recognize the misguided policies of decades that led to World War II. And you can recognize the imperialism of both sides as a product of their time. There are those who, by this means, excuse Thomas Jefferson's slavery. If we can do that, perhaps we can also excuse Franklin Roosevelt's war. But that doesn't mean we should be making plans to repeat either one of those things.

III. WAR IS NOT GOING TO END ON ITS OWN

If war were ending on its own, it would be ending because people were causing it to end. That trend could be reversed if enough people found out that anti-war work was succeeding and took that as a reason to stop engaging in it. But we are not yet clearly succeeding. If we want to end war we will have to redouble our efforts and get many more people involved. First, let's examine the evidence that war is not fading away.

Counting Bodies

Over the centuries and decades, death counts have grown dramatically, shifted heavily onto civilians rather than combatants, and been overtaken by injury counts as even greater numbers have been injured but medicine has allowed them to survive. Deaths are now due primarily to violence rather than to disease, formerly the biggest killer in wars. Death and injury counts have also shifted very heavily toward one side in each war, rather than being evenly divided between two parties.

Understanding that there are countless shortcomings in any comparisons across wars fought in different epochs, using different technologies, operating under different conceptions of law, etc., here are some comparisons that nonetheless seem useful. The following is, of course, a sampling and not intended in any way as a comprehensive discussion of all U.S. or global wars.

In the U.S. War for Independence, some 63,000 died, including 46,000 Americans, 10,000 British, and 7,000 Hessians. Possibly 2,000 French died on the American side in North America, and more fighting the British in Europe. The British and the U.S. each had about 6,000 wounded. Civilians were not killed in significant numbers in battle, as they are in modern war. But the war likely caused a smallpox epidemic, which took 130,000 lives. It is noteworthy that more Americans died than did those on the other side, that more died than were wounded and lived, that more soldiers died than civilians, that the United States won, that the war was fought within the United States, and that no refugee crisis was created (although the gate was opened wide to genocide of Native Americans and other future wars).

In the War of 1812, some 3,800 U.S. and British soldiers died fighting, but disease brought the death total to some 20,000. The number of wounded was smaller, as it would be in most wars before penicillin and other medical advances arrived for World War II and later wars. Until then, more soldiers died of their wounds. The fighting in the War of 1812 did not kill large numbers of civilians. More Americans died than did those on the other side. The war was fought within the United States, but the war was a failure. Canada was not conquered. On the contrary, Washington D.C. was burned. No major refugee crisis resulted.

U.S. wars against Native Americans were one part of a genocide. According to the U.S. Census Bureau in 1894, "The Indian wars under the government of the United States have been more than 40 in number. They have cost the lives of about 19,000 white men, women and children, including those killed in individual combats, and the lives of about 30,000 Indians." These were wars fought within the United States, which the U.S. government "won" more often than it lost, and in which the other side suffered the greater share of deaths, including significant deaths inflicted on civilians. A refugee crisis of major proportions was one of the primary results. In several ways, these wars are a closer model for later U.S. wars than other early wars are.

In the U.S. war on Mexico of 1846-1848, 1,773 Americans were killed in action, while 13,271 died from sickness, and 4,152 were wounded in the conflict. Approximately 25,000 Mexicans were killed or wounded. Once again, disease was the big killer. Again, more died than were wounded and survived. Fewer Americans died than did those on the other side. More soldiers died than civilians. And the United States won the war.

In each of the wars described above, the casualty figures were larger percentages of the overall populations at the time than they are of populations today. Whether and how that makes the wars worse than the absolute casualty counts suggest is a matter for debate. Adjusting for population does not have as significant an effect as one might think. The U.S. population at the time of its war on Mexico was almost as big as Iraq's population at the time of Shock and Awe. The United States lost 15,000. Iraq lost 1.4 million. To be more precise, the U.S. population was about 22 million and Mexico's about 2 million, of whom some 80,000 were in the territories seized by the United States. Those 80,000 saw their nationality changed, although some were permitted to remain

Mexican. Iraq saw millions made homeless, including millions forced to travel outside Iraq and live as refugees in foreign lands.

The U.S. Civil War, which grew out of the war on Mexico and other factors, stands apart. The death count is usually estimated at something remarkably close to the 654,965 Iraqis killed as of June 2006, as reported by Johns Hopkins. One researcher lists the Civil War casualties as follows:

Total military dead: 618,022, including 360,022 Northern and 258,000 Southern. For the North, 67,058 died in combat, 43,012 from wounds, 219,734 from disease, including 57,265 from dysentery, and 30,218 died as prisoners of war. For the South, 94,000 died in combat, an unknown number from wounds, 138,024 from disease, and 25,976 as prisoners of war. Another 455,175 were wounded, including 275,175 from the North and 180,000 from the South.

More recent research, using census data, estimates the U.S. Civil War dead at 750,000. Estimations and speculation place civilian deaths, including from starvation, at an additional 50,000 or more. A U.S. population of 31.4 million in 1860, reduced by 800,000, means a loss of 2.5 percent, or less than half what Iraq lost in OIL (Operation Iraqi Liberation, the war's original name); 1,455,590 killed out of 27 million is a loss of 5.4 percent.

The U.S. Civil War numbers finally begin to approach the death toll of major modern wars, while still remaining relatively evenly divided between the two sides. In addition, the numbers wounded begin to surpass the numbers dead. Yet, the killing remains mainly the killing of soldiers, not civilians.

The first U.S. overthrow of a foreign government beyond the destruction of the Native American nations was in Hawaii in 1893. Nobody died, and one Hawaiian was wounded. These overthrows would never again be so bloodless.

The U.S. wars on Cuba and the Philippines at the end of the nineteenth century begin to move us in a new direction. These were violent occupations on foreign soil. Disease remained a big killer, but it impacted one side disproportionately, because the conflict was taking place far from the shores of the occupier.

The Spanish-American War was fought in Cuba, Puerto Rico, and Guam, but not in the United States. The war on the Philippines was fought in the Philippines. In the Spanish-American War, the United States saw 496 killed in action, 202 died of wounds, 5,509 died from disease, and 250 were killed by the United States' own (presumably accidental) destruction of the *USS Maine* prior to the war. The Spanish saw 786 killed in action, 8,627 died of wounds, and 53,440 died from disease. The Cubans saw another 10,665 dead.

But it is in the Philippines that the death count, as well as the length of the war, really begins to look familiar. The United States had 4,000 killed, mostly by disease, plus 64 from Oregon (not yet part of the United States). The Philippines had 20,000 combatants killed, plus 200,000 to 1,500,000 civilians dead from violence and diseases, including cholera. Over 15 years, by some estimates, the

United States' occupying forces, together with disease, killed over 1.5 million civilians in the Philippines, out of a population of 6 to 7 million. That's less than a quarter the size of the Iraqi population, with a similar sized slaughter imposed on it, over a period roughly twice as long. A population of 7 million losing 1.5 million lives is losing a staggering 21 percent of its population—making this war, by that standard, if the high-end estimate of deaths is correct, the worst war the United States has engaged in, apart from the Native American genocide. The U.S. death count of 4,000 in the Philippines is very similar to the U.S. death count in Iraq. From here on out, U.S. death counts will be smaller than those on the other side, and military death counts will be smaller than civilian. Victories also become questionable or temporary.

The First World War saw some 10 million military deaths, about 6 million of them on the side of Russia, France, the British, and other Allies. About a third of those deaths were due to the Spanish influenza. About 7 million civilians were killed in Russia, Turkey, Germany and elsewhere by violence, famine, and disease. The "Spanish" flu epidemic was largely created by the war, which increased transmission and augmented mutation; the war may also have increased the lethality of the virus. That epidemic killed 50 to 100 million people worldwide. The Armenian genocide and wars in Russia and Turkey arguably grew out of this war, as arguably did World War II. Ultimately, total death counts are impossible. But we can note that this war involved direct and indirect killing on a larger scale, that the direct killing was relatively evenly balanced between the two sides, and that the surviving wounded now outnumbered those killed.

This was intense, rapid killing that took place in the space of just over 4 years, rather than an occupation as lengthy as those of Iraq or Afghanistan in the 21st century. But the direct deaths were spread over dozens of nations. The highest death count by nation was 1,773,300 in Germany, followed by 1,700,000 in Russia, 1,357,800 in France, 1,200,000 in Austria-Hungary, 908,371 in the British Empire (actually many nations), and 650,000 in Italy, with no other nation's casualties rising above 350,000. The 1.7 million killed in Germany were taken from a population of 68 million. The 1.7 million killed in Russia were taken from a population of 170 million. Iraq lost a similar number of lives in its recent "liberation," but from a population of only 27 million. Yet, somehow we think of World War I as a senseless horror of truly staggering proportions, and of the liberation of Iraq as a regime change that didn't go very well—or even as a shining success.

WWII is the worst single thing humanity has done to itself in any relatively short period of time. Setting aside the catastrophic side effects and repercussions from which we may never recover (any more than U.S. troops may ever leave Germany or Japan), the absolute number of people killed—some 50 to 70 million—easily tops the list. Measured as a percentage of global population killed, World War II is surpassed only by very lengthy series of events like the fall of Rome. The impact of World War II on particular nations varied dramatically, ranging from 16 percent of the population of Poland killed, all the way down to 0.01 percent of the population of Iraq killed. About 12 nations lost more than 5 percent of their population in World War II. Japan lost 3 percent to 4 percent. France and Italy lost 1 percent each. The U.K. lost less than 1 percent. The United States lost 0.3 percent. Nine nations in World War II lost a million or more lives. Among those that did not were France, Italy, the U.K., and the U.S. So, the more recent war in Iraq was worse for Iraq than many nations' experience in World War II. We can also conclude without a shadow of doubt that the damage done to nations' population is not what determines the number of Hollywood movies made about one war rather than another.

With World War II we entered the era in which civilian deaths outnumber military deaths. About 60 percent to 70 percent of the deaths were civilian, a figure that includes victims of bombing and all other violence including the holocaust and ethnic cleansing campaigns, as well as disease and famine. (You can find numerous sources on the Wikipedia page on "World War II Casualties".) We also entered the era in which killing can very disproportionately impact one side. What Germany did to the Soviet Union and Poland, and what Japan did to China account for the vast bulk of the dying. Thus the victorious allies suffered the greater share. We also entered the era in which the wounded outnumber the dead, and the era in which war deaths come primarily from violence rather than disease. And we opened the door to a tremendous escalation in U.S. military presence and operations around the globe, an escalation that is ongoing.

The war on Korea, which has ever officially ended, in its initial intense years killed an estimated 1.5 to 2 million civilians, North and South, plus nearly a million military dead on the side of the North and China, a quarter million or more military dead from the South, 36,000 dead from the United States, and much smaller numbers from several other nations. The military wounded far outnumbered the military dead. As in World War II, some two-thirds of the deaths were civilian, and U.S. deaths were few compared with others. Unlike World War II, there was no victory; that was the beginning of a trend that would last.

The war on Vietnam was Korea, but worse. There was a similar lack of victory and a similar number of U.S. casualties, but a larger number of deaths for the people who lived in the battlefield. The U.S. dead turn out to have accounted for 1.6 percent of the dying. That compares to about 0.3 percent in Iraq. A 2008 study by Harvard Medical School and the Institute for Health Metrics and Evaluation at the University of Washington estimated 3.8 million violent war deaths, combat and civilian, north and south, during the years of U.S. involvement in Vietnam. The civilian deaths outnumbered the combat deaths, again amounting to about two-thirds of total deaths. The wounded were in much higher numbers, and judging by South Vietnamese hospital records, one-third were women and one-quarter children under age 13. U.S. casualties included 58,000 killed and 153,303 wounded, plus 2,489 missing. (Medical advances help explain the ratio of wounded to killed; subsequent medical advanced and body armor advances may help explain why U.S. deaths in Iraq were not at a level similar to U.S. deaths in Korea or Vietnam.) The 3.8 million out of a population of 40 million is nearly a 10 percent loss, or twice what OIL did to Iraq. War spilled into neighboring countries. Refugee crises ensued. Environmental damage and delayed deaths, often due to Agent Orange, continue to this day.

One Big Atrocity

The more recent war on Iraq, measured purely in terms of deaths, may compare favorably to the war on Vietnam, but the details of how the killing was done are remarkably similar, as shown in Nick Turse's *Kill Anything That Moves*. Turse documents that policy decisions handed down from the top led consistently, over a period of years, to the ongoing slaughter of millions of civilians in Vietnam. Much of the killing was done by hand or with guns or artillery, but the lion's share came in the form of 3.4 million combat sorties flown by U.S. and South Vietnamese aircraft between 1965 and 1972.

The well-known My Lai massacre in Vietnam was not an aberration. Turse documents a pattern of atrocities so pervasive that one is compelled to begin viewing the war itself as one large atrocity. Similarly, endless atrocities and scandals in Afghanistan and Iraq are not aberrations even though U.S. militarists have interpreted them as freak occurrences having nothing to do with the general thrust of the war.

"Kill anything that moves," was an order given to U.S. troops in Vietnam indoctrinated with racist hatred for the Vietnamese. "360 degree rotational fire" was a command given on the streets of Iraq to U.S. troops similarly conditioned to hate, and similarly worn down with physical exhaustion.

Dead children in Vietnam elicited comments like "Tough shit, they grow up to be VC." One of the U.S. helicopter killers in Iraq heard in the "Collateral Murder" video says of dead children, "Well it's their fault for bringing their kids into a battle." President Obama's campaign senior adviser Robert Gibbs commented on a 16-year-old American killed by a U.S. drone in Yemen: "I would suggest that you should have a far more responsible father if they are truly concerned about the well being of their children." The "they" may mean foreigners or Muslims or just this particular man. The murder of the son is disgracefully justified by reference to his father. In Vietnam anyone dead was the enemy, and sometimes weapons would be planted on them. In drone wars, any dead males are militants, and in Iraq and Afghanistan weapons have often been planted on victims (See IVAW.org/WinterSoldier). After U.S. troops killed pregnant women in a night-raid in Afghanistan, they dug the bullets out with knives and blamed the killings on the women's family members. (See *Dirty Wars* by Jeremy Scahill.)

The U.S. military during the Vietnam War shifted from keeping prisoners toward murdering prisoners, just as the current war has shifted from incarceration toward murder with the change in president from Bush to Obama. (See "Secret 'Kill List' Proves a Test of Obama's Principles and Will," *New York Times*, May 29, 2012.) In Vietnam, as in Iraq, rules of engagement were broadened until the rules allowed shooting at anything that moved. In Vietnam, as in Iraq, the U.S. military sought to win people over by terrorizing them. In Vietnam, as in Afghanistan, whole villages were eliminated.

In Vietnam, refugees suffered in horrible camps, while in Afghanistan children have frozen to death in a refugee camp near Kabul. Torture was common in Vietnam, including water-boarding. But at that time it hadn't yet been depicted in a Hollywood movie or television show as a positive occurrence. Napalm, white phosphorus, cluster bombs, and other widely despised and banned weapons were used in Vietnam, as they are in the global war on terra [*sic*]. Vast environmental destruction was part of both wars. Gang rape was a part of both wars. The mutilation of corpses was common in both wars. Bulldozers flattened people's villages in Vietnam, not unlike what U.S.-made bulldozers do now to Palestine.

Mass murders of civilians in Vietnam, as in Iraq and Afghanistan, tended to be driven by a desire for revenge. (See *Kill Anything That Moves* by Nick Turse.) New weaponry allowed U.S. troops in Vietnam to shoot long distances, resulting in a habit of shooting first and investigating later, a habit now developed for drone strikes. Self-appointed teams on the ground and in helicopters went "hunting" for natives to kill in Vietnam as in Afghanistan. And of course, Vietnamese leaders were targeted for assassination.

Vietnamese victims who saw their loved ones tortured, murdered, and mutilated are—in some cases—still furious with rage decades later. It's not hard to calculate how long such rage will last in the nations now being "liberated."

Recent Wars

Throughout the centuries, overlapping with the larger wars I've been describing, the U.S. has engaged in numerous smaller wars.

These wars continued between the U.S. withdrawal from Vietnam and the U.S. invasion of Iraq. An example is the 1983 invasion of Grenada. Grenada lost 45 lives and Cuba 25, the United States 19, with 119 U.S. wounded. Another example is the U.S. invasion of Panama in 1989. Panama lost between 500 and 3,000, while the U.S. lost 23 lives.

The United States assisted Iraq in its war on Iran during the 1980s. Each side lost hundreds of thousands of lives, with Iran suffering perhaps two-thirds of the deaths.

Operation Desert Storm, 17 January 1991 – 28 February 1991, killed some 103,000 Iraqis, including 83,000 civilians. It killed 258 Americans (making them 0.25 percent of the dead), although disease and injuries showed up in the years that followed. At the end of the war 0.1 percent of participating U.S. troops were considered killed or wounded, but by 2002, 27.7 percent of veterans were listed as dead or wounded, many diagnosed with Gulf War Syndrome.

As of September 2013, the U.S. war on Afghanistan was ongoing, with U.S. defeat inevitable. As with Iraq, it has a back-story of death and destruction dating back many years—in this case at least to what Zbigniew Brzezinski admitted was a U.S. effort to provoke a Soviet invasion in 1979. U.S. deaths in Afghanistan since 2001 are about 2,000, plus 10,000 wounded. Additionally there are much greater numbers of troops with brain injuries and post traumatic stress disorder (PTSD). During some years, suicides have outpaced combat deaths. But, as in other modern wars, the occupied nation has suffered most of the injuries and deaths, including about 10,000 Afghan security forces killed, 200 Northern Alliance forces killed, and tens or hundreds of thousands of civilians killed violently, plus as many as hundreds of thousands or millions dead from nonviolent results of the war including freezing, starvation, and disease. Afghanistan's refugee crisis has been expanded by millions during the current occupation, while U.S. missile strikes in northern Pakistan have created another 2.5 million refugees.

Documentation for all of the above statistics can be found at WarIsACrime.org/Iraq along with an analysis of the casualty studies in Iraq which places the most likely total there at 1,455,590 excess deaths. These are deaths above the high death rate that existed in 2003, following the worst sanctions and longest bombing campaign in history.

U.S. drone strikes in Pakistan, Yemen, and Somalia are producing significant numbers of deaths, almost all of them on one side. These numbers come from TheBureauInvestigates.com:

PAKISTAN
CIA Drone Strikes in Pakistan 2004–2013
Total US strikes: **372**
Total reported killed: **2,566-3,570**
Civilians reported killed: **411-890**
Children reported killed: **167-197**
Total reported injured: **1,182-1,485**

YEMEN

US Covert Action in Yemen 2002–2013

Confirmed US drone strikes: 46-56

Total reported killed: **240-349**

Civilians reported killed: **14-49**

Children reported killed: **2**

Reported injured: **62-144**

Possible extra US drone strikes: 80-99

Total reported killed: **283-456**

Civilians reported killed: **23-48**

Children reported killed: **6-9**

Reported injured: **81-106**

All other US covert operations: 12-77

Total reported killed: **148-377**

Civilians reported killed: **60-88**

Children reported killed: **25-26**

Reported injured: **22-111**

SOMALIA

US Covert Action in Somalia 2007–2013

US drone strikes: 3-9

Total reported killed:**7-27**

Civilians reported killed: **0-15**

Children reported killed: **0**

Reported injured: **2-24**

All other US covert operations: 7-14

Total reported killed: **47-143**

Civilians reported killed: **7-42**

Children reported killed: **1-3**

Reported injured: **12-20**

The high end of these counts totals 4,922, remarkably close to the figure of 4,700 that Senator Lindsey Graham has made public—without, however, explaining where he got it. These numbers compare very favorably to Operation Iraqi Liberation (meaning they are smaller), but making that comparison may be dangerous. The U.S. government did not replace a ground war or a traditional bombing campaign with a drone war in the countries above. It created drone wars where it would have been very unlikely to create any wars at all, in the absence of drones. It created these drone wars while escalating a massive occupation in Afghanistan of which drone kills were only one element.

Looking at the wars of the earth's leading war-making nation, measured by death counts, the wars do not seem to be on a path toward ending. If only drone wars are fought in the future, that could mean a reduction in death counts. But it would not mean an end to wars, and therefore it would be difficult to guarantee that wars would be limited in any manner—wars being very difficult beasts to control once started.

The chart below displays the estimated number of people killed in major U.S. wars over the years, from oldest on the left to most recent on the right. I've included major wars and left out many quite minor ones, both early and more recent. I've not included wars against Native Americans, primarily because they were spread over such a long period of time. I've also not included the sanctions that came in between the Gulf War and the Iraq War, even though they killed more people than the Gulf War did. I've included only the relatively brief bursts of killing that we commonly call wars. And

I've included deaths on all sides, including those killed by disease during a war, but not post-war epidemics, and not injuries. The injured who survived were few in the wars at the left. The injured were more than the dead in the wars at the right.

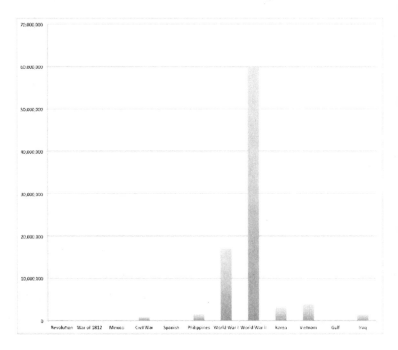

The chart below is the same as the chart above, only with the two world wars removed. Those two wars took place in so many different nations and killed on such an enormous scale, that it is easier to compare the other wars if they are omitted. Common references to the Civil War as the deadliest U.S. war appear wildly off when looking at this chart; that's because this chart—unlike most U.S. news media—includes the deaths on both sides of foreign wars. I have not tried to break each column into combatants and civilians, a practically difficult and morally dubious operation, but one that would inevitably show civilian deaths heavily present only on the right-hand side of the chart. I have also not separated U.S. from foreign deaths. Doing so would result in the five wars toward the left being colored all or significantly a color representing U.S. deaths, and the five wars on the right being colored almost entirely a color representing foreign deaths, with a little sliver indicating U.S. deaths as part of the total.

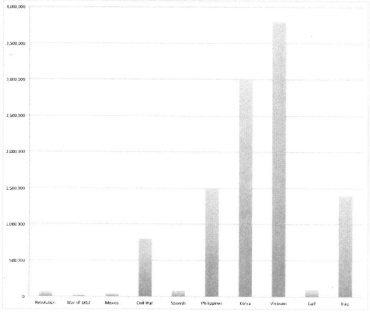

The third chart, on the next page, displays, not the number of deaths, but the percent of a population killed. One might have assumed that the earlier wars saw fewer deaths because the populations of the countries involved were smaller. However, when we adjust for population, the chart doesn't change very much. The earlier wars still appear less deadly than the later wars. The populations used for this calculation are the populations of the countries where the wars were fought: the United States for the revolution and the civil war, the United States and Canada for the war of 1812, the United States and Mexico for the Mexican-American war, Cuba and Puerto Rico and Guam for the Spanish-American war, the Philippines or Korea or Vietnam for the wars bearing those nations' names, and Iraq for the last two wars.

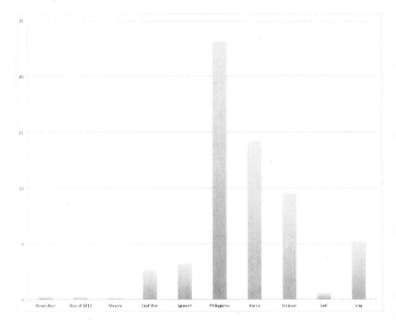

Counting Dollars

When Americans hear "the cost of war" they often think of two things: dollars and U.S. soldiers' lives. During the G.W.O.T. (global war on terror/terra) Americans have not been asked to sacrifice, to cut back, to pay more taxes, or to contribute to the cause. In fact, they've had their taxes reduced, especially if they have large incomes or are among the population of "corporate persons." (Wealth concentration is a common result of wars, and these wars are no exception.) U.S. people have not been drafted for military or other duty, except through the poverty draft and the deceptions of the military recruiters. But this lack of sacrifice hasn't meant no financial cost. Below is a menu of past wars and price tags in 2011 dollars. The trend seems to be moving mostly in the wrong direction.

- War of 1812 - $1.6 billion
- Revolutionary War - $2.4 billion
- Mexican War - $2.4 billion
- Spanish-American War - $9 billion
- Civil War - $79.7 billion
- Persian Gulf - $102 billion
- World War I - $334 billion
- Korea - $341 billion
- Afghanistan - $600 billion
- Vietnam - $738 billion
- Iraq - $810 billion
- Total post-9/11 - $1.4 trillion
- World War II - $4.1 trillion

Joseph Stiglitz and Linda Bilmes in 2008 calculated the true total cost of OIL (the Iraq War) as three to five trillion (higher now that the war went on for years longer than they expected). That figure includes impacts on oil prices, future care of veterans, and—notably—lost opportunities.

Brown University's "Cost of War" Project garnered attention in 2013 by claiming that the U.S. cost for the war on Iraq would be $2.2 trillion. A few clicks into their website one finds this: "Total US federal spending associated with the Iraq war has been $1.7 trillion through FY2013. In addition, future health and disability payments for veterans will total $590 billion and interest accrued to pay for the war will add up to $3.9 trillion." The $1.7 trillion plus the $0.59 trillion equals the $2.2 trillion placed in the headline of the report. The additional $3.9 trillion in interest has been left out. And, even though Brown is taking its data from papers by Linda Bilmes, it leaves out numerous considerations that were included in Bilmes' and Stiglitz' book *The Three Trillion Dollar War*, including most notably the impact of the war on fuel prices and the impact of lost opportunities. Adding those to the $6.19 trillion listed here would make the estimate of $3 to $5 trillion in Bilmes' and Stiglitz' book look as "conservative" as they said it was.

Measured in dollars, as in deaths, wars by the nation most invested in wars right now don't show any long-term trends toward disappearance. Instead, wars appear to be a constant, enduring, and growing presence.

Who Says War Is Vanishing?

Most influentially, the argument that war is going away has been made by Steven Pinker in his book *The Better Angels of Our Nature: Why Violence Has Declined*. But it is an argument that can be found in various forms in the work of numerous Western academics.

War, as we have seen above, is not actually going away. One way to suggest that it is involves conflating war with other varieties of violence. The death penalty seems to be going away. Spanking and whipping children seems to be going away in some cultures. And so on. These are trends that should help convince people of the case I made in Part I above: War can be ended. But these trends say nothing about war actually being ended.

The fictional account of war going away treats Western civilization and capitalism as forces for peace. This is done, in large part, by treating Western wars on poor nations as the fault of those poor nations. The U.S. war in Vietnam was the fault of the Vietnamese who weren't enlightened enough to surrender as they should have. The U.S. war in Iraq ended with Bush's declaration of "mission accomplished!" after which the war was a "civil war" and the fault of the backward Iraqis and their lack of Western capitalism. And so on.

Missing from this account is the relentless push for more wars in the U.S., Israeli, and other governments. U.S. media outlets routinely discuss "the next war" as if there simply must be one. Missing is the development of NATO into a global aggressive force. Missing is the danger created by the proliferation of nuclear technology. Missing is the trend toward greater corruption of elections and governance, and the growing—not shrinking—profits of the military industrial complex. Missing is the expansion of U.S. bases and troops into more nations; as well as U.S. provocations toward China, North Korea, Russia, and Iran; increases in military spending by China and many other nations; and misconceptions about past wars including the recent war in Libya and proposals for wider war in Syria.

Wars, in the view of Pinker and other believers in war's vanishing, originate in poor and Muslim nations. Pinker indicates no awareness that wealthy nations fund and arm dictators in poor countries, or that they sometimes "intervene" by dropping that support and dropping bombs along with it. Also likely countries to make war are those with ideologies, Pinker tells us. (As everyone knows, the United States has no ideology.) "The three deadliest postwar conflicts," Pinker writes, "were fueled by Chinese, Korean, and Vietnamese communist regimes that had a fanatical dedication to outlasting their opponents." Pinker goes on to blame the high death rate in Vietnam on the willingness of the Vietnamese to die in large numbers rather than surrender, as he thinks they should have.

The U.S. war on Iraq ended, in Pinker's view, when President George W. Bush declared "mission accomplished," since which point it was a civil war, and therefore the causes of that civil war can be analyzed in terms of the shortcomings of Iraqi society. "[I]t is so hard," Pinker complains, "to impose liberal democracy on countries in the developing world that have not outgrown their superstitions, warlords, and feuding tribes." Indeed it may be, but where is the evidence that the United States government has been attempting it? Or the evidence that the United States has such democracy itself? Or that the United States has the right to impose its desires on another nation?

Early in the book, Pinker presents a pair of charts aimed at showing that, proportionate to population, wars have killed more prehistoric and hunter-gatherer people than people in modern states. None of the prehistoric tribes listed go back earlier than 14,000 BCE, meaning that the vast majority of human existence is left out. And these charts list individual tribes and states, not pairs or groups of them that fought in wars. The absence of war through most of human history is left out of the equation, dubious statistics are cited for earlier wars, those statistics are compared to the global population rather than the population of the tribes involved, and—significantly—the deaths counted from recent U.S. wars are only U.S. deaths. And they're measured against the population of the United States, not the nation attacked. At other times, Pinker measures war deaths against the population of the globe, a measure that doesn't really tell us anything about the level of devastation in the areas where the wars are fought. He also omits indirect or delayed deaths. So the U.S. soldiers killed in Vietnam get counted, but those killed more slowly by Agent Orange or PTSD do not get counted. Of course spears and arrows used in ancient wars did not have the same delayed effects as Agent Orange. U.S. soldiers killed in Afghanistan get counted by Pinker, but the greater number who die a bit later from injuries or suicide do not.

Pinker acknowledges the danger of nuclear proliferation only in a very glass-half-full kind of way:

If one were to calculate the amount of destruction that nations have actually perpetrated as a proportion of how

> *much they could perpetrate, given the destructive capacity*
> *available to them, the postwar [meaning post-World War II]*
> *decades would be many orders of magnitude more peaceable*
> *than any time in history.*

So, we're more peaceful because we've built more deadly weapons!

And civilization's progress is good because it progresses.

And yet, after all the fancy footwork calculating our path to peace, we look up and see bloodier wars than ever before, and machinery in place to wage more of them—machinery accepted as unquestionable or literally unnoticed.

Our Wars Aren't Bad Like Your Wars

Pinker isn't alone. Jared Diamond's latest book, *The World Until Yesterday: What We Can Learn from Traditional Societies*, suggests that tribal people live with constant war. His math is as fuzzy as Pinker's. Diamond calculates the deaths from war in Okinawa in 1945, not as a percentage of Okinawans, but as a percentage of all the combatant nations' populations, including the population of the United States, where the war was not fought at all. With this statistic, Diamond claims to prove that World War II was less deadly than violence in an "uncivilized" tribe.

Daniel Jonah Goldhagen's *Worse Than War: Genocide, Eliminationism, and the Ongoing Assault on Humanity* argues that genocide is distinct from war and worse than war. By this means, he redefines portions of wars, such as the U.S. firebombing of Japan or the Nazi holocaust, as not war at all. The portions of wars that are left in the category of war are then justified. For Goldhagen, the war on Iraq was not mass-murder because it was just. The 9/11 attacks were genocide, despite their smaller scale, because unjust. When Saddam Hussein killed Iraqis it was mass murder, but when the United States killed Iraqis it was justified. (Goldhagen doesn't comment on U.S. assistance to Hussein in killing Iraqis.)

Goldhagen argues that ending war should be a lower priority than ending mass murder. But without his Western blinders, war looks like a type of mass murder. War is, in fact, the most acceptable, respectable, and widest spread form of mass-murder around. Making war unacceptable would be a huge step in the direction of making all killing unacceptable. Keeping war in place as a "legitimate" foreign policy tool guarantees that mass murder will continue. And redefining much of what war consists of as non-war fails dramatically at making the case that war is going away.

"There Is Evil in the World"

A common response to arguments for abolishing war is. "No. No. No. You need to understand that there is evil in the world. The world is a dangerous place. There are bad people in the world." And so forth. The act of pointing out this obvious piece of information suggests a very deep acceptance of war as the only possible response to a troubled world, and a complete conviction that war is not itself something evil. Opponents of war do not, of course, believe there is nothing evil in the world. They just place war in that category, if not at the very top of it.

It is the unthinking acceptance of war that keeps war going. Campaigning for president, Hillary Clinton said that if Iran were to launch a nuclear attack against Israel, she would "totally obliterate" Iran. She meant this threat as deterrence, she said. (See video at WarIsACrime.org/Hillary.) At the time, the Iranian government said, and U.S. intelligence agencies said, that Iran had no nuclear weapons and no nuclear weapons program. Iran had nuclear energy, pushed on it decades earlier by the United States. Of course, Iran's theoretical obliteration of Israel would be just as evil as a U.S. obliteration of Iran. But the United States really does have the capability to launch nuclear weapons at Iran and has repeatedly threatened to do so, with both the Bush and Obama White Houses showing great affection for the phrase "All options are on the table." They shouldn't be. Such threats should not be made. Talk of obliterating nations should be left behind us. That sort of talk makes it much more difficult to make peace, to truly engage with another nation, to move relations forward to the point where no nation imagines that another is going to develop a horrible weapon and use it.

The MIC

Authors who view war as ending, and as a third-world phenomenon, tend to miss some of the major contributing factors to war, including those encompassed by the phrase "military industrial complex." These factors include the skill of propagandists, the open bribery and corruption of our politics, and the perversion and impoverishment of our educational and entertainment and civic engagement systems that lead so many people in the United States to support and so many others to tolerate a permanent state of war in search of enemies and profits despite decades-long demonstrations that the war machine makes us less safe, drains our economy, strips away our rights, degrades our environment, distributes our income ever upward, debases our morality, and bestows on the wealthiest nation on earth miserably low rankings in life-expectancy, liberty, and the ability to pursue happiness.

None of these factors are insurmountable, but we won't surmount them if we imagine the path to peace is to impose our superior will on backward foreigners by means of cluster bombs and napalm meant to prevent primitive atrocities.

The military industrial complex is a war-generating engine. It can be dismantled or transformed, but it is not going to stop generating wars on its own without a big push. And it is not going to stop just because we come to the realization that we would really, really like it to stop. Work is going to be required.

A couple of years ago, National Public Radio interviewed a weapons executive. Asked what he would do if the hugely profitable occupation of Afghanistan were to end, he replied that he hoped there could be an occupation of Libya. He was clearly joking. And he didn't get his wish—yet. But jokes don't come from nowhere. Had he joked about molesting children or practicing racism his comments would not have aired. Joking about a new war is accepted in our culture as an appropriate joke. In contrast, mocking war as backward and undesirable is just not done, and might be deemed incomprehensible, not to mention unfunny. We have a long way to go.

IV. WE HAVE TO END WAR

If we want war to end, we are going to have to work to end it. Even if you think war is lessening, it won't continue doing so without work. And as long as there is any war, there is a significant danger of widespread war. Wars are notoriously hard to control once begun. With nuclear weapons in the world (and with nuclear plants as potential targets), any war-making carries a risk of apocalypse. War-making and war preparations are destroying our natural environment and diverting resources from a possible rescue effort that would preserve a habitable climate. As a matter of survival, war and preparations for war must be completely abolished, and abolished quickly.

We need a movement that differs from the past movements that have been against each successive war or against each offensive weapon. We need a movement, as Judith Hand and Paul Chappell and David Hartsough and many others have proposed, for the elimination of war in its entirety. We need education, organization, and activism. And we need structural changes to make these steps more powerful.

Ending war-making by the United States and its allies would go a very long way toward ending war globally. For those of us living in the United States, at least, the place to start ending war is within our own government. We may be able to work on this together with people living near U.S. military bases—which is a fairly large percentage of the people on earth.

Ending U.S. militarism wouldn't eliminate war globally, but it would eliminate the pressure that is driving several other nations to increase their military spending. It would deprive NATO of its leading advocate for and greatest participant in wars. It would cut off the largest supply of weapons to Western Asia (a.k.a. the Middle East) and other regions. It would remove the major barrier to a reunification of Korea. It would create U.S. willingness to support arms treaties, join the International Criminal Court, and allow the United Nations to move in the direction of its stated purpose of eliminating war. It would create a world free of nations threatening first-use of nukes, and a world in which nuclear disarmament might proceed more rapidly. Gone would be the last major nation using cluster bombs or refusing to ban land mines. If the United States kicked the war habit, war itself would suffer a major and possibly fatal set-back.

So, how do we get there from here?

We need a shift in our culture away from acceptance of war, and we need supportive changes that help us get there. Resistance to a U.S. war on Syria at the time of this writing has seen smaller rallies than were held in 2003 against a U.S.-led war on Iraq, but greater support in the polls, greater support within the military and the government, and greater understanding by elected officials. This is in part the result of the past decade of organizing and educating. A lot of work that has seemed futile to people at the time has been paying off in terms of a shift in public attitude, almost a re-birth of the Vietnam Syndrome, if not quite the anti-war enlightenment of the 1920s.

Taking the profitability out of war, and the corruption out of elections, are separate steps from educating people in war abolition. But they are steps likely to make abolition easier. Creating a Department of Peace or otherwise making diplomatic options more prominent is another step. Improvements to our communications and education systems as a whole will be improvements to a movement for peace. The development of independent media, and steps to break up the corporate media cartel are critical for ending war. Student and cultural exchanges with people from nations on the Pentagon's likely target list (Syria, Iran, North Korea, China, Russia, etc.) will go a long way toward building resistance toward those potential future wars.

We need to remember to think, not in terms of forces that supposedly create war on their own directly, but in terms of factors that contribute to the social acceptability of war in our culture. One of our primary targets therefore is false beliefs, propaganda, a broken communications system. War does not necessarily produce racism, and racism does not necessarily produce war. But racist thinking makes some of our friends and neighbors more accepting of wars against different-looking people. Of course, we need to abolish racism anyway, apart from its contribution to militarism. But a campaign to abolish war needs to take on racism's contribution to it without imagining that war simply follows from racism (a notion that could divert the entire anti-war campaign into an anti-racism campaign).

The same logic applies to many other factors. If evidence suggests that poor child raising and poor education contribute to people's subservience to authority or support for violent public policies, then those factors need to be addressed, as they should be addressed anyway for numerous reasons. But in a campaign to abolish war no factor can take the place of advocacy for the abolition of war. Capitalism, in a certain form, may be a factor contributing to war-making, but war predates capitalism by millennia. Ideas about masculinity and heroism may be contributing to militarism, but ever since war ceased to involve hand-to-hand combat, there has been nothing intrinsically masculine about the duties of soldiers. Women and homosexuals have been integrated into the U.S. military much more smoothly than the military predicted. We don't need to undo maleness, but altering certain ways of thinking about male respectability would almost certainly help. It sounds laughable, but the leading argument for attacking Syria in August-September 2013 amounted to a defense of President Obama's manhood, in as much as he had previously threatened "consequences" if chemical weapons were used.

This may change somewhat as wars come to be fought by robots. We may stop thinking of the driving force behind war as the nature of the beings on the front lines. We would be right to go ahead and change our thinking now. The driving force behind wars lies with those at the top of the government, and with all of us who let them get away with their behavior.

With this understanding, we should target all or parts of xenophobia, nationalism, religion, extreme materialism, fear, greed, hatred, false-pride, blind obedience, environmental destructiveness, lack of empathy, lack of community, the praise of the military, the lack of praise for resisters and objectors, militaristic conceptions of masculinity, and every other factor that seems to be contributing to the acceptance of war. These efforts will only succeed in combination with a direct nonviolent assault on the acceptance of war—which is what this book is intended to be a part of. And success in eliminating the acceptance of war will go a great distance in the other direction, toward helping to reduce fear, xenophobia, environmental destructiveness, etc.

I can't say for sure whether empowering women—I mean en masse, not tokenism—would discourage war. The United States yielded the vote to women long before Switzerland did, and we know which nation has been more bellicose. But clearly reforms that empower everyone equally and disempower any elite will help our efforts against the war machine. Empowering everyone equally will mean empowering women. And empowering women will move any society in the direction of empowering everyone equally.

Other reforms will benefit all kinds of activism, including anti-war activism. Moving money from big banks to cooperatives, encouraging worker ownership of workplaces, and developing local economic and political structures will help. While we need an international rule of law, we don't need the transfer of most governmental functions further away from people, but rather the reverse. We need greater democracy from the local level on up, with greater local control over much of public policy.

Closing prisons—another institution in dire need of an abolition movement—would certainly help. Many potential activists are locked up, and many actual activists are threatened as though they were criminals. Ceasing to prescribe drugs to children who challenge authority couldn't hurt. Less television, fewer video games, more time away from cell phones—all of that could make a difference. Greater economic security, if we can get it, could help as well—although desperation also has its advantages as a mobilizer of activism.

Reforms in our way of thinking about ourselves and our responsibilities are key. We should understand the extent to which our opinions are shared by others. Usually we are far less alone than we imagine. Often we are a majority depicted as a tiny minority by the media. (Most of us oppose U.S. war-making in Syria, but televised political shows suggest falsely that virtually everyone disagrees with us.) We should understand, also, how effective activism often has been. And we should learn to act from a non-partisan position of strength, without self-censorship or pre-compromise.

The Danger of Obedience

War support often consists largely of support for the idea of trusting and obeying presidents and other officials. Even people who routinely denounce the dishonesty and depravity of politicians, when it comes to war (and its aura of nationalism) insist that we accept outrageous policies on the basis of wildly implausible claims put forth on the basis of secret evidence kept from us supposedly for our own good. Obedience is seen as a virtue in the military, and people not in the military begin to talk as if it is their virtue as well. They begin referring to their "commander in chief" rather than their president. They begin believing that citizens should shut up and do as they're told and think as they're told to think, rather than running the country and compelling public servants to serve the public. "You're with us or against us," they say, forgetting that one can demand accountability from one's government without necessarily supporting a violent invasion by a foreign power.

Obedience is a danger. If a two-year-old is about to run in front of a car, please do yell "stop!" and hope for as much obedience as possible. But when you grow up, your obedience should always be conditional. If a master chef appears to be instructing you to prepare a revoltingly bad dinner but wants you to obey his or her instructions on faith, you might very well choose to do so, considering the risk to be tolerable. If, however, the chef tells you to chop off your little finger, and you do it, that will be a sure sign that you've got an obedience problem.

This is not a trivial or comical danger. The majority of volunteers in experiments are willing to inflict what they believe is severe pain or death on other human beings when a scientist tells them to do so for the good of science. These are usually known as Milgram experiments, and the pain or death is faked by actors. Were an actor pretending to be a scientist to tell volunteers to cut off their little fingers, I bet they wouldn't do it. But they are willing to do far worse to someone else. The good old Golden Rule is a counter to this deficiency, but so is resistance to blind obedience. Most suffering in the world is not created by independent individuals, but by large numbers of people obeying when they should be resisting.

Chelsea Manning's legal defense team tried to explain her exposing of numerous crimes by the government as the result of her "post-adolescent idealism" almost as if that were a disease. But many thousands of people had access to the same information and failed to make it public. Surely we could, with more reason, diagnose them as suffering from Blind Obedience Disorder.

Remember the regretful drone pilot discussed above. His tragedy was not an experiment, but all too real. We should think about how not to put ourselves in positions in which we are expected to blindly obey. It is possible to find jobs that don't include that unhealthy expectation. And we should prepare ourselves to refuse immoral instructions whenever we receive them, including above all the instruction to sit back and do nothing.

Governments Pretend to Ignore Activism

Several years ago a lot of people were protesting the U.S. war in Iraq. The president and most of Congress and most of the big media outlets were busy giving out the impression that such protests were ignored or even counter-productive. But former president George W. Bush's memoirs recall a leading Republican senator secretly telling him the pressure was becoming too great and they'd need to end the war. Bush signed an agreement with the government of Iraq to leave in three years.

In 1961 the USSR was withdrawing from a moratorium on nuclear testing. A protest at the White House urged President Kennedy not to follow suit. Posters read "Kennedy, Don't Mimic the Russians!" One protester recalled their action for decades as having been pointless and futile, until he found an oral history interview with Adrian Fisher, deputy director of the U.S. Arms Control and Disarmament Agency. Fisher said that Kennedy had delayed resuming testing because of the protest.

A delay in a policy we oppose is not as good as a permanent ban, but if those protesters had known they were being listened to they would have come back day after day and brought their friends and possibly achieved that permanent ban. That they imagined they weren't being listened to appears ridiculous if you read enough history. People are always listened to, but those in power go to great lengths to give the impression of not paying any serious attention.

Lawrence Wittner interviewed Robert "Bud" McFarlane, President Ronald Reagan's former national security advisor, asking him whether the White House had paid much attention to protests demanding a "freeze" in nuclear weapons building. "Other administration officials had claimed that they had barely noticed the nuclear freeze movement," Wittner said. "But when I asked McFarlane about it, he lit up and began outlining a massive administration campaign to counter and discredit the freeze—one that he had directed. ... A month later, I interviewed Edwin Meese, a top White House staffer and U.S. attorney general during the Reagan administration. When I asked him about the administration's response to the freeze campaign, he followed the usual line by saying that there was little official notice taken of it. In response, I recounted what McFarlane had revealed. A sheepish grin now spread across this former government official's face, and I knew that I had caught him. 'If Bud says that,' he remarked tactfully, 'it must be true.'"

It's funny: even when protesting government lies or government secrecy, people tend to fall for the lie that the government is ignoring you. Yet, in 2011, when a relatively tiny movement began to take to the streets under the banner of "Occupy," the government rolled out a massive effort of infiltration, eavesdropping, harassment, brutality, and propaganda—while, of course, claiming to have noticed nothing and done nothing about something so unworthy of notice.

Large companies and government contractors take activism just as seriously. Reporter Steve Horn recently reported on fracking (gas extraction) companies studying the U.S. military's "counterinsurgency manual" for purposes of developing psychological operations ("psy-ops") against environmental activists. Horn also reported on documents from the Stratfor corporation outlining its extensive efforts to counter nonviolent activism. A number of corporations exist just for that purpose.

Those in power don't restrict themselves to directing you toward inaction. They also work on moving you toward doing lots of things that seem effective but aren't. The way to keep the nation safe, they say, is to go shopping! Or lobby for this watered-down pathetic piece of legislation! Or devote all your activist energy to election campaigning, and then go home and collapse in exhaustion as soon as the election is over—exactly when you should be gearing up to demand actions out of whoever won the election. These activities that have little impact are depicted as serious and effective, while activities that historically have had tremendous real impact (organizing, educating, demonstrating, protesting, lobbying, heckling, shaming, nonviolently resisting, producing art and entertainment, creating alternative structures) are depicted as disreputable and ineffective and lacking in seriousness. Don't be fooled!

Of course, being active is much more fun than not. Of course, the influence you have is always possible even if undetected (you might inspire a child who goes on to do great things years later, or slightly win over an opponent who takes a few more years to fully see the light). Of course, we have a moral duty to do everything we can regardless of the ease of success. But I'm convinced we'd see a lot more activism if people knew how much they are listened to. So tell them! And let's remember to keep telling ourselves.

Doing Nothing Is Obeying A Deadly Order

Imagine writing a story about a village that faces possible destruction, and the people don't do anything to prevent it.

That's not how stories are written.

But that's the world we live in and fail to recognize.

We are being instructed to sit at a desk and zap the earth to death, and we're compliantly zapping away. Only the zapping doesn't look like zapping; it looks like living. We work and eat and sleep and play and garden and buy junk at the store and watch movies and go to baseball games and read books and make love, and we don't imagine we can possibly be destroying a planet. What are we, *the Death Star?*

But a sin of omission is morally and effectively equivalent to a sin of commission. We need to be saving the earth and we're not doing so. We're allowing global warming and other major environmental destruction to roll ahead. We're allowing militarization and war-making to advance. We're watching the concentration of wealth. We see the division of society into castes. We know we're building prisons and drones and highways and pipelines and missiles while closing schools and condemning our grandparents to poverty. We are aware that we're funding military bases and multi-billionaires with our hard work while fueling mass suffering, bitterness, rage, frustration, and violence.

We see these worsening cycles and we sit still. Don't sit still. Sitting still is mass-murder. Don't obey anyone who tells you to sit still. Don't search for or wait for a leader. Don't sell your conscience to a group or a slogan or a political party.

What Then Must We Do?

We must create a moral movement against mass-murder, even when the mass-murder is accompanied by flags or music or assertions of authority and promotion of irrational fear. We must not oppose one war on the grounds that it isn't being run well or isn't as proper as some other war. We must not focus entirely on the harm wars do to the aggressors. We must acknowledge the victims. We must see one-sided slaughters for what they are and grow appropriately outraged. A "good war" must sound to all of us, like it sounds to me, as no more possible than a benevolent rape or philanthropic slavery or virtuous child abuse. "You can no more win a war than you can win an earthquake," said Jeanette Rankin, the heroic congresswoman who voted against U.S. entry into both world wars.

A new film called *The Ultimate Wish: Ending the Nuclear Age* shows a survivor of Nagasaki meeting a survivor of Auschwitz. It is hard in watching them meeting and speaking together to remember or care which nation committed which horror. We should get to the point where we can see all war with that same clarity. War is a crime not because of who commits it but because of what it is.

We must make war abolition the sort of cause that slavery abolition was. We must work around or undo the corporate media. We must develop faith in ourselves and our power. We must be fearless. We must mock war as dueling was mocked. We must abandon the idea that we can be for peace without opposing wars. We must abandon the idea that we can oppose wars without opposing the entire machinery and worldview of war-making. We must hold up resisters, conscientious objectors, peace advocates, diplomats, whistleblowers, journalists, and activists as our heroes. We must thank them for their service. We must honor them. We must cease honoring those who participate in war or war industries.

We must develop alternative avenues for heroism and glory, including nonviolent activism, and including serving as peace workers and human shields in places of conflict. Little is more important than advancing common understanding of nonviolence as an alternative form of conflict to violence, and ending the habit of thinking that one can ever be faced with only the choices of engaging in violence or doing nothing.

We must stop trying to discover a good patriotism, and begin thinking beyond borders. We must abandon nationalism without supposing that we are then somehow obliged to hate our nation any more than we hate our state or city when we fail to encourage our state or city to engage in warfare. We must make a concerted effort to remove nationalism, xenophobia, racism, religious bigotry, and U.S. exceptionalism (the idea that what we would condemn if another nation did it is acceptable when the U.S. government does it) from our thinking.

We must oppose wars for rational, fact-based reasons, as opposed to fictions and misperceptions. Opposing a war because of the party a president belongs to, or because we'd rather not be so generous to the war's potential victims ("I don't want to bomb Syria. After everything we did for Iraq, the Iraqis still aren't grateful") is good as far as it goes. But this attitude promotes falsehoods about the actual effects of U.S. war and sanctions on Iraq and strengthens the belief that some other war will be worth supporting.

Lies: The Worst Ones Come After a War

Lies are told before, during, and after wars, and it is those told after the wars that teach future generations that wars are acceptable. Without lies about past wars, future wars would never be contemplated at all, not even as "a last resort." Without lies about World War II and its predecessors, there would have been no war on Korea or Vietnam. Without lies about those conflicts, there would have been no U.S. wars since.

Not to minimize the importance of exposing the lies told just prior to a new war, we need to recognize that those lies stand on the shoulders of all the accumulated myths and disinformation about previous wars. When President Obama escalated the war on Afghanistan, he claimed that an escalation in Iraq had been a "success". The Pentagon is investing $65 million right now in a "Vietnam Commemoration Project" to transform that catastrophe into a noble cause. On the 60th anniversary of the armistice in Korea, President Obama declared that war a "victory." Millions of people were killed in Korea to accomplish exactly nothing, and 60 years later the commander in chief feels obliged to redefine that as a victory. The Iraq War is also being beautified, even as you read these words.

Former speech writer for President George W. Bush, David Frum said on March 5, 2013: "The Iraq war has led to a huge shift in regional oil production. Iraq is returning to world oil markets, massively. Last year Iraq produced more oil than in any year since the first Gulf War. By some estimates, Iraq will soon overtake

Russia as the world's number-two oil exporter. Iran meanwhile has dropped out of the top 10 oil-exporting countries. Iraq's return to world oil markets has enabled the sanctions that have pushed Iran out. If Iraq were still ruled by Saddam Hussein, it's hard to imagine that the western world would dare take its present hard line against Iran. And of course, if Saddam Hussein had remained in power after 2003, he too would have had the benefit of $100/barrel with which to finance his regime's military ambitions."

The war on Iraq is here justified because it has facilitated threatening war on Iran and sanctioning Iran, as well as because a failure to remove Saddam Hussein would mean that he would still be around, unless perhaps the United States had never supported him in the first place.

Having established that the war was good, Frum tries to gain credibility by gently critiquing the way it was "managed": "The war was expensive and badly managed. It did real damage to the international credibility of the United States. ... It left 4,000 Americans dead and many thousands more seriously wounded. Had we known all this in advance, the war would not have been fought. But it would be wrong to say the war achieved nothing. And it's wrong to shut our eyes to the ugly consequences of leaving Saddam in power."

Doing so might distract us from shutting our eyes to the ugly consequences of our sociocide, our utter destruction of Iraqi society. From Frum's comments you'd imagine the war killed 4,000 people, not 1.4 million.

Bill Bigelow, curriculum editor of Rethinking Schools, which has just released a book called *Teaching About the Wars,* wrote in March 2013:

Now, as we celebrate the 10th anniversary of the U.S. invasion of Iraq, our wars in the Middle East have moved from the front pages of our newspapers to the insides of our textbooks. The huge corporations that produce those texts have no interest in nurturing the kind of critical thought that might generate questions about today's vast inequalities of wealth and power—or, for that matter, about the interventionist policies of our government. Exhibit A is Holt McDougal's Modern World History *on the U.S. war with Iraq, which might as well have been written by Pentagon propagandists. Maybe it was. In an imitation of Fox News, the very first sentence of the Iraq war section mentions the 9/11 attacks and Saddam Hussein side by side. The book presents the march to invasion as reasonable and inevitable, while acknowledging: 'Some countries, France and Germany, called for letting the inspectors continue searching for weapons.' That's the only hint of any opposition to war, despite the fact that there was enormous popular opposition to the war, culminating on February 15, 2003, the date which saw millions of people around the world demand that the United States not invade Iraq—if you're keeping track, this was the largest protest in human history, according to the Guinness Book of World Records.*

This, of course, is a pattern in corporate textbooks: Conflate governments with the people; ignore social movements. After a quick and bloodless description of the fall of Saddam Hussein's regime, the textbook's final section is headlined 'The Struggle Continues.' It begins: 'Despite the coalition victory, much work remained in Iraq.' The only thing missing from this rah-rah section is the confetti: 'With the help of U.S. officials, Iraqis began rebuilding their nation.' Oh, is that how it happened? Significantly, there is no Iraqi quoted in the entire section—itself one of the most powerful lessons here. It's a primer in legitimating imperialism: the violent and squabbling Third World others get no say; we will decide what's good for them. In a mockery of the term 'critical,' the chapter closes with four 'Critical Thinking & Writing' exercises. Here is the sole 'critical writing' activity: 'Imagine you are a speechwriter for President Bush. Write the introductory paragraph of a speech to coalition forces after their victory in Iraq.'

We're turning our children into David Frum. We need activism in our schools to reverse this trend.

Public Opinion, Without Action, Cannot Prevent Another War

We need improved schools and improved news reporting, because we need better informed opinions. Then we need to turn those opinions into effective action. The polls were very useful in August-September 2013 in holding off, at least temporarily, an attack on Syria. But they would have done us no good without the hard work of thousands of people and hundreds of groups. Countless rallies, demonstrations, protests, lobby visits, public forums, interviews, and a flood of emails and phone calls made the will of the public visible and pinned Congress members down on a position for peace.

We need, and we are building, a movement that is international. We need allies around the world. We need their help, and they need ours, in eliminating nuclear weapons, weaponized drones, cluster bombs, and other instruments of death, as well as in closing military bases, and shutting down the School of the Americas at Fort Benning, Ga., where so many assassins and torturers have been trained. These partial steps toward war abolition should be understood as just that. We should use them to build the abolition movement. We should measure our progress in terms of how many people say Yes, we can end war, and Yes, we should end war.

We must build a coalition that can accomplish serious steps: defunding military advertising campaigns, restoring war powers to the legislative branch, cutting off weapons sales to dictatorships, etc. To do this, we'll want to bring together all those sectors that rightfully ought to be opposing the military industrial complex: moralists, ethicists, preachers of morality and ethics, doctors, psychologists, and protectors of human health, economists, labor unions, workers, civil libertarians, advocates for democratic reforms, journalists, historians, promoters of transparency in public decision-making, internationalists, those hoping to travel and be liked abroad, environmentalists, and proponents of everything worthwhile on which war dollars could be spent instead: education, housing, arts, science, etc. That's a pretty big group.

But most activist organizations want to stay focused in their niches. Many are reluctant to risk being called unpatriotic. Some are tied up in profits from military contracts. We must work our way around these barriers.

We have, in recent years, begun to see some environmentalist organizations oppose some military base construction (such as on Jeju Island, South Korea), some civil liberties groups object to an entire mode of warfare (drone wars), some labor unions back a process of conversion from war industries to peace industries, and various cities and the U.S. Conference of Mayors demand a reduction in military spending. These are the tiny pebbles from which we must start building a massive wall of opposition to war-making. We must move organizations away from exclusively treating the symptoms—as when civil liberties groups oppose torture or indefinite imprisonment—and toward also attempting to cure the root cause: militarism.

Green energy has far greater potential to handle our energy needs (and wants) than is commonly supposed, because the massive transfer of money that would be possible with the abolition of war isn't usually considered. We should encourage environmentalists to begin thinking in those terms. War making is not good for the economy as a whole. There are wealthy interests not profiting from weaponry or other war spending, and not profiting from a militarily enforced exploitation of foreign peoples. A U.S.-

based green energy company ought to be able to back a process of conversion from war spending to green-energy spending. As should the rest of us. In 2013, the state of Connecticut created a commission to work on converting manufacturing in Connecticut from a war to a peace basis. This effort was backed by and has the involvement of workers and owners, as well as peace advocates. If it does well, it should be closely observed by the other 49 states and the nation as a whole.

Celebrity War Games

In 2012, if you watched the Olympics on NBC, you saw advertisements promoting a war-o-tainment reality show cohosted by retired U.S. General Wesley Clark, co-starring Todd Palin, and with no apparent role for reality. The ads bragged about the use of real bullets, but the chances that any of the celebrities engaged in "war competition" on NBC's "Stars Earn Stripes" were going to be shot and killed was essentially what it was for John Wayne as he promoted war while dodging it (even if nuclear weapons testing got him in the end). RootsAction.org set up a website at StarsEarnStripes.org to pressure NBC (and its war-profiteering owner, General Electric) to show the real costs of war. During the 1999 bombing of Yugoslavia commanded by Gen. Wesley Clark, civilians and a TV station were bombed, while cluster bombs and depleted uranium were used.

A coalition formed to denounce "Stars Earn Stripes." Activists protested at NBC's studios in New York. Nine Nobel Peace Prize laureates spoke out against the program. The show became an embarrassment and was quickly canceled (or, as NBC put it, not produced beyond its "pilot" episodes). We need that sort of public response to every new outrage, and to outrages that have been around so long we barely notice them anymore.

A Process Toward Peace

Just as people often believe that we have to choose between bombing the hell out of a country or doing nothing, people often believe we have to choose between continuing to routinely bomb the hell out of countries or dismantling the entire military by Wednesday. Instead, we should envision a disarmament process that can proceed over a period of months and years. Disarmament will encourage further disarmament. Foreign aid (not the weaponry we call "foreign aid") and cooperation will discourage hostility. Compliance with the rule of law will encourage the development of international law enforcement. I use the term "enforcement" not to suggest the use of war but rather the prosecution of individual war makers.

Partial steps along the way may prove useful. A campaign to ban weaponized drones could take advantage of the fact that drone strikes look more like murder to many people than do other forms of murder in war. But such campaigns should be used to advance the larger goal of war abolition, and not to encourage the idea of improving or sanitizing war. A campaign to ban military bases in foreign nations might also be a good place to gain a foothold.

As we begin to imagine a war-free world, what will we see?

Virginia and West Virginia don't go to war because they are both the United States. France and Germany don't go to war because they are both Europe. One is tempted to say that nations would not go to war if they were united by an earth-wide government. But, in fact, a global government as corrupt and unaccountable— or more so—than our national governments would not help us. We need to build healthy democratic representation from the local level up to an international federation. Getting there may actually mean distributing more power to localities, states, and regions, rather than concentrating more power at higher levels.

The United Nations should be reformed or replaced. It should be made democratic, stripping away the special privileges for a handful of nations. It should be made into a complete opponent of war. Acceptance of defensive or U.N.-authorized wars should be undone. One way to do this would be to revive understanding of the Kellogg-Briand Pact, which pre-dates the U.N. Charter and remains on the books of over 80 nations, with others free to sign on.

Outlawing War

When people propose banning war by law, including by Constitutional amendment, I have mixed reactions. While banning war is just what the world ordered, it has about it something of the whole Bush-Cheney ordeal during which we spent years trying to persuade Congress to ban torture. By no means do I want to be counted among those opposed to banning torture. But it is relevant, I want to suggest, that torture had already been banned.

Torture had been banned by treaty and been made a felony, under two different statutes, before George W. Bush was made president. In fact, the pre-existing ban on torture was stronger and more comprehensive than any of the loophole-ridden efforts to re-criminalize it. Had the debate over "banning torture" been entirely replaced with a stronger demand to prosecute torture, we might be better off today. (As I was writing this, on July 24, 2013, Congressman Alan Grayson passed an amendment to a military spending bill once again "banning torture.")

We are in that same situation with regard to war. War was banned 85 years ago, making talk of banning war problematic. We were in that same situation, in fact, even before the U.N. Charter was drafted 69 years ago. By any reasonable interpretation of the U.N. Charter, most—if not all—U.S. wars are forbidden. The United Nations did not authorize the invasion of Afghanistan or Iraq, the overthrow of the Libyan government, or the drone wars in Pakistan or Yemen or Somalia. And by only the wildest stretch of the imagination are these wars defensive from the U.S. side. But the two loopholes created by the U.N. Charter (for defensive and U.N.-authorized wars) are severe weaknesses. There will always be those who claim that a current war is in compliance with the U.N. Charter or that a future war might be. So, when I say that war is illegal, I don't have the U.N. Charter in mind.

Nor am I thinking that every war inevitably violates the so-called laws of war, involving countless atrocities that don't stand up under a defense of "necessity" or "distinction" or "proportionality," although this is certainly true. Banning improper war, while useful as far as it goes, actually supports the barbaric notion that one can conduct a proper war. The situation in which a war would be a "just war" is as mythical as the much-imagined situation in which torture would be justified.

Nor do I mean that U.S. Constitutional war powers are violated or fraud is perpetrated in making the case for war, although these and other violations of law are frequent companions of U.S. wars.

I also do not want to dispute the advantages of banning war in the highest U.S. law, the Constitution. There is a common misconception that holds up lesser, statutory law as more serious than the Constitution or the treaties that it makes "supreme law of the land." This is a dangerous inversion. The whistleblower Edward Snowden is right to expose violations of the Fourth Amendment. Senator Dianne Feinstein is wrong to insist that those violations have been legalized by statutes—which is debatable even if one accepts unconstitutional statutes. Amending the Constitution to ban war would (if the Constitution were complied with) prevent any lesser law from legalizing war.

But a treaty would do that too. And we already have one.

It is little known and even less appreciated that the United States is party to a treaty that bans all war. This treaty, known as the Kellogg-Briand Pact, or the Peace Pact of Paris, or the Renunciation of War, is listed on the U.S. State Department's website. The Pact reads:

> *The High Contracting Parties solemnly [sic] declare in the*
> *names of their respective peoples that they condemn recourse*
> *to war for the solution of international controversies, and*
> *renounce it, as an instrument of national policy in their*
> *relations with one another.*

> *The High Contracting Parties agree that the settlement or*
> *solution of all disputes or conflicts of whatever nature or of*
> *whatever origin they may be, which may arise among them,*
> *shall never be sought except by pacific means.*

Pacific means only. No martial means. No war. No targeted murder. No surgical strikes.

The story of how this treaty, to which over 80 nations are party, came to be is inspiring. (See my book, *When the World Outlawed War*.) The peace movement of the 1920s is a model of dedication, patience, strategy, integrity, and struggle. Playing a leading role was the movement for "outlawry," for the outlawing of war. War had been legal until that point, as people falsely imagine it to be today.

Eliminating war, the outlawrists believed, would not be easy. A first step would be to ban it, to stigmatize it, to render it unrespectable. A second step would be to establish accepted laws for international relations. A third would be to create courts with the power to settle international disputes. The outlawrists took the first big step in 1928, with the treaty taking effect in 1929. We haven't followed through. In fact we've collectively buried what was probably the single biggest news story of 1928: the creation of this treaty.

With the creation of the peace pact, wars were avoided and ended. But armament and hostility continued. The mentality that accepts war as an instrument of national policy would not vanish swiftly. World War II came. And, following World War II, President Franklin Roosevelt used the Kellogg-Briand Pact to prosecute the losers of the war, not just for "war crimes," but also for the brand new crime of war. Despite an endless plague of war on and among the poor nations of the world, the wealthy armed nations have yet to launch a third world war among themselves.

When not simply ignored or unknown, the Kellogg-Briand Pact is dismissed because World War II happened. But what other legal ban on undesired behavior have we ever tossed out following the very first violation and what appears to have been a quite effective prosecution? An argument can also be made that the U.N. Charter undoes the earlier pact simply by coming later in time. But this is by no means an easy argument, and it requires understanding the U.N. Charter as the re-legalization of war rather than the ban on war that most people imagine it to be.

In fact, the Kellogg-Briand Pact has been used in cases of international law long after the adoption of the U.N. Charter, including a case at the World Court in 1998 that arguably prevented a U.S. war against Libya. (See Francis Boyle's *Destroying Libya and World Order*.)

In the two years since I published an account of the activism that created the Pact, I have found a great deal of interest in reviving awareness of it. People may not be as sick of war now as they were following World War I, or at least not as open to the possibility of abolition, but many are pretty far down that road. Groups and individuals have launched petitions. The St. Paul, Minnesota, City Council (where Frank Kellogg lived) has voted to create a peace holiday on August 27th, the day the treaty was signed in 1928 in a scene well described in the song *Last Night I Had the Strangest Dream.*

A fan of the story has created an essay contest that's received thousands of entries. Drone protesters have educated judges about the Peace Pact when they've been hauled into court for making use of the First Amendment. A Congress member has put into the Congressional Record his recognition that the Kellogg-Briand Pact made war illegal. I just saw an op-ed in the *New York Times* by some law professors mentioning the pact. And I've been in touch with other nations not party to the treaty and not party to any wars, encouraging them to both sign on to the Pact and then urge certain other parties to begin complying with it.

When someone wants to legalize torture or campaign bribery they point to court proceedings marginalia, overridden vetoes, speeches, and tangentially related ancient precedents. When we want to de-legalize war, why not point to the Kellogg-Briand Pact? It is a treaty to which the United States is party. It is the Supreme Law of the Land. It not only does what we want. It does more than most people dare to dream. I've found that some people are inspired by the Pact's existence and by the fact that our great-grandparents were able to create a public movement that brought it into existence.

War the Crime, not "War Crimes"

It is common to think of "war crimes" as improper conduct during a war, but not to think of the war itself as a crime. This needs to change. When presidents and other leaders of nations get away with launching wars, their successors repeat their crimes.

Many of us pushed hard for the impeachment or prosecution of George W. Bush, predicting that without that accountability his crimes would be continued and repeated. Lately I've been, somewhat bitterly, remarking, "Wow, not impeaching Bush has sure paid off!" His successor has continued and expanded upon many of his war powers and policies.

Many loyal Republicans opposed impeaching George W. Bush. So did most liberal and progressive activist groups, labor unions, peace organizations, churches, media outlets, journalists, pundits, organizers, and bloggers, not to mention most Democratic members of Congress, most Democrats dreaming of someday being in Congress, and—toward the end of the Bush presidency—most supporters of candidate Barack Obama or candidate Hillary Clinton.

Remarkably in the face of this opposition, a large percentage and sometimes a majority of Americans told pollsters that Bush should be impeached. It's not clear, however, that everyone understood why impeachment was needed. Some might have supported a successful impeachment of Bush and then turned around and tolerated identical crimes and abuses by a Democrat.

But this is the point: whoever followed Bush's impeachment would have been far less likely to repeat and expand on his high crimes and misdemeanors. And the reason many of us wanted Bush impeached—as we said at the time—was to prevent that repetition and expansion, which we said was virtually inevitable if impeachment was not pursued.

"You just hate Republicans" was the most common argument against impeachment, but there were others. "It's more important to elect someone different." "Why do you want President Cheney?" "Why do you want President Pelosi?" "Why distract from good work?" "Why put the country through trauma?" "Why not focus on ending war?" "Why not do investigations?" "Why divide the Democrats?" "Why start a process that can't succeed?" "Why destroy the Democratic Party the way impeaching Clinton destroyed the Republican Party?" We answered these questions as patiently as possible at great length and enormous repetition for years and years (See WarIsACrime.org/ImpeachFAQ).

People pursued alternatives to impeachment, from spreading the word about how bad the crimes and abuses were, to pushing legislation to redundantly re-criminalize Bush's criminal behavior, to promoting supposedly lesser-evil candidates, to promoting truly good candidates, to constructing ways to drop out of society and wash one's hands of it. The trouble was that when you let a president make war, and everything that comes with war—spying without warrant, imprisoning without charge, torture, lying, secrecy, rewriting laws, persecuting whistleblowers—you can predict, as we predicted for years, that the next president will adopt and build on the same policies. Nothing short of punishing the offender will deter the successor.

In fact, the new president, working with Congress and all of his other facilitators, has turned abuses into policies. The scandal and secretiveness have been replaced with executive orders and legislation. Crimes are now policy choices. Checking off lists of murder victims is official open policy. (See "Secret 'Kill List' Proves a Test of Obama's Principles and Will," *New York Times*, May 29, 2012.) Secret laws are normal. Secretly rewritten laws are established practice. Spying in violation of the Fourth Amendment is openly defended and "legalized," with sporadic bursts of public outrage and establishment excusing, following new detailed revelations. Whistleblowing is being transformed into treason.

What failure to impeach Bush has done to legitimize his crimes is nothing compared to what it has done to delegitimize impeachment. If a tyrannical president who liberals hated and who talked funny and who didn't even pretend to be killing for some higher benevolent purpose can't be impeached, then who can? Surely not an intelligent, articulate African American who pretends to agree with us and gives speeches denouncing his own policies!

But this is the same problem as before. Making speeches against Bush's abuses was not enough. Clapping for speeches against

Obama's abuses—even speeches by Obama—is not enough. There is a reason why people abuse power. Power corrupts them. And absolute power corrupts them absolutely. Telling a handful of Congress members who are forbidden to speak about it, and most of whom don't really give a damn, what sort of outrages you are up to is not a system of checks and balances or the rule of law.

Refusal to impeach pulls the foundation out from under representative government. Congress won't impeach for violation of subpoenas, so it avoids issuing subpoenas, and it therefore can't compel production of witnesses or documents, so it doesn't take a position on an important matter, so the unofficial U.S. state media takes no position either, and people follow the media.

There is no demand to impeach Obama alive among the public as I write this. There are murmurs about impeaching him for minor or fictional crimes, but not for war. In an ideal world, we would compel Congress to truly drop the partisanship and proceed with a double-impeachment of Obama and Bush for identical crimes. (Impeachments after leaving office are possible and have been done; do a web search for "William Belknap".)

We should aim to bring about that ideal world, in which top officials are held accountable for crimes, and the most serious crime on the list is the crime of war.

A Global Rescue Plan

People ask: Well, what do we do about the terrorists?

We begin learning history. We stop encouraging terrorism. We prosecute suspected criminals in courts of law. We encourage other nations to use the rule of law. We stop arming the world. And we take a little fraction of what we spend killing people and use it to make ourselves the most beloved people on the planet.

The United States alone is perfectly capable, if it chooses, of enacting a global marshall plan, or—better—a global rescue plan. Every year the United States spends, through various governmental departments, roughly $1.2 trillion on war preparations and war. Every year the United States foregoes well over $1 trillion in taxes that billionaires and centimillionaires and corporations should be paying.

If we understand that out-of-control military spending is making us less safe, rather than more—just as Eisenhower warned and so many current experts agree—it is clear that reducing military spending is a critical end in itself. If we add to that the understanding that military spending hurts, rather than helping, economic well-being, the imperative to reduce it is that much clearer.

If we understand that wealth in the United States is concentrated beyond medieval levels and that this concentration is destroying representative government, social cohesion, morality in our culture, and the pursuit of happiness for millions of people, it is clear that taxing extreme wealth and income are critical ends in themselves.

Still missing from our calculation is the unimaginably huge consideration of what we are not now doing but easily could do. It would cost us $30 billion per year to end hunger around the world. We just, as I was writing this, spent nearly $90 billion for another year of the "winding down" war on Afghanistan. Which would you rather have: three years of children not dying of hunger all over the earth, or year #13 of killing people in the mountains of central Asia? Which do you think would make the United States better liked around the world?

It would cost us $11 billion per year to provide the world with clean water. We're spending $20 billion per year on just one of the well-known useless weapons systems that the military doesn't really want but which serves to make someone rich who controls Congress members and the White House with legalized campaign bribery and the threat of job elimination in key districts. Of course, such weapons begin to look justified once their manufacturers begin selling them to other countries too. Raise your hand if you think giving the world clean water would make us better liked abroad and safer at home.

For similar affordable amounts, the United States, with or without its wealthy allies, could provide the earth with education, programs of environmental sustainability, encouragement to empower women with rights and responsibilities, the elimination of major diseases, etc. The Worldwatch Institute has proposed spending $187 billion annually for 10 years on everything from preserving topsoil ($24 billion per year) to protecting biodiversity ($31 billion per year) to renewable energy, birth control, and stabilizing water tables. For those who recognize the environmental crisis as another critical demand as urgent in its own right as the war-making crisis, the plutocracy crisis, or the unmet human needs crisis, a global rescue plan that invests in green energy and sustainable practices appears even more powerfully to be the moral demand of our time.

War-ending, earth-saving projects could be made profitable, just as prisons and coal mines and predatory lending are made profitable now by public policy. War-profiteering could be banned or rendered impractical. We have the resources, knowledge, and ability. We don't have the political will. The chicken-and-egg problem traps us. We can't take steps to advance democracy in the absence of democracy. A female face on an elite ruling class won't solve this. We can't compel our nation's government to treat other nations with respect when it has no respect even for us. A program of foreign aid imposed by imperial-minded arrogance won't work. Spreading subservience under the banner of "democracy" won't save us. Imposing peace through armed "peace-keepers" prepared to kill won't work. Disarming only so-much, while continuing to suppose that a "good war" might be needed, won't get us far. We need a better view of the world and a way to impose it on officials who can be made to actually represent us.

Such a project is possible, and understanding how easy it would be for powerful officials to enact a global rescue plan is part of how we can motivate ourselves to demand it. The money is available several times over. The globe we have to rescue will include our own country as well. We don't have to suffer more than we are suffering now in order to greatly benefit others. We can invest in health and education and green infrastructure in our own towns as well as others' for less than we now dump into bombs and billionaires.

Such a project would do well to consider programs of public service that involve us directly in the work to be done, and in the decisions to be made. Priority could be given to worker-owned and worker-run businesses. Such projects could avoid an unnecessary nationalistic focus. Public service, whether mandatory or voluntary, could include options to work for foreign and internationally run programs as well as those based in the United States. The service, after all, is to the world, not just one corner of it. Such service could include peace work, human shield work, and citizen diplomacy. Student exchange and public-servant exchange programs could add travel, adventure, and cross-cultural understanding. Nationalism, a phenomenon younger than and just as eliminable as war, would not be missed.

You may say I'm a dreamer. We number in the hundreds of millions.

Educate, Organize, Get Active

Give this book to a friend or relative who doesn't agree with it.

Give it to your Congress member, your library, and your crazy uncle.

Invite me to come talk with your group about it.

Don't have a group? Join or create one. I recommend checking out and getting involved with the groups found on the following websites. These groups do not necessarily recommend this book or have anything to do with it, but I recommend them:

DavidSwanson.org

WarIsACrime.org

RootsAction.org

VCNV.org

WarResisters.org

VeteransForPeace.org

CodePink.org

Space4Peace.org

UNACPeace.org

UnitedForPeace.org

StopWar.org.uk

AntiWar.org

PeacePeople.com

AFutureWithoutWar.org

WILPFUS.org

WagingPeace.org

NuclearResister.org

SOAW.org

IPB.org

NobelWomensInitiative.org

HistoriansAgainstWar.org

Peace-Action.org

ThePeaceAlliance.org

Acknowledgments

Special thanks to Leah Bolger, William Blum, Steve Cobble, Jeff Cohen, Nicolas Davies, Mike Ferner, Glen Ford, Judith Hand, John Horgan, Kathy Kelly, Jim O'Brien, Coleen Rowley, Robert Shetterly, Alice Slater, Linda Swanson, and Lawrence Wittner. None of them is responsible for anything that, despite their best efforts, I still managed to get wrong. Thanks also to Medea Benjamin for finding the cover photo by Scott Strazzante which I purchased from the *Chicago Tribune*. This book also benefitted from discussions with numerous people at the War Resister's League's 90th Year Convention at Georgetown University in Washington, D.C., in August 2013, and at the Democracy Convention and the Veterans For Peace Convention, both held in Madison, Wis., in August 2013.

About David Swanson

David Swanson's books include: *War Is A Lie* (2010), *When the World Outlawed War* (2011), and *The Military Industrial Complex at 50* (2011), as well as *Daybreak: Undoing the Imperial Presidency and Forming a More Perfect Union* (2009) and a children's book, *Tube World* (2012). Swanson hosts the weekly syndicated radio show *Talk Nation Radio*. He has been a journalist, activist, organizer, educator, and agitator. Swanson helped plan the nonviolent occupation of Freedom Plaza in Washington, D.C., in 2011. Swanson holds a master's degree in philosophy from the University of Virginia. He has worked as a newspaper reporter and as a communications director, with jobs including press secretary for Dennis Kucinich's 2004 presidential campaign, media coordinator for the International Labor Communications

Association, and three years as communications coordinator for ACORN, the Association of Community Organizations for Reform Now. He blogs at DavidSwanson.org and WarIsACrime.org and works as Campaign Coordinator for the online activist organization RootsAction.org. Swanson also works on the communications committee of Veterans For Peace, of which he is an associate (non-veteran) member. Swanson is Secretary of Peace in the Green Shadow Cabinet.

About Kathy Kelly

Kathy Kelly co-coordinates Voices for Creative Nonviolence (VCNV.org), a campaign to end U.S. military and economic warfare. During each of 12 recent trips to Afghanistan, as an invited guest of the Afghan Peace Volunteers, Kelly has lived alongside ordinary Afghan people in a working class neighborhood in Kabul. She and her companions in VCNV believe that "where you stand determines what you see." Kelly has also joined with activists to protest drone warfare by holding demonstrations outside of U.S. military bases in Nevada, upstate New York, and Missouri. From 1996 to 2003, VCNV activists formed 70 delegations that openly defied economic sanctions by bringing medicines to children and families in Iraq. Kathy and her companions lived in Baghdad throughout the 2003 "Shock and Awe" bombing. They have also lived alongside people during warfare in Gaza, Lebanon, Bosnia and Nicaragua. Kelly was sentenced to one year in federal prison for planting corn on nuclear missile silo sites (1988-89) and spent three months in prison, in 2004, for crossing the line at Fort Benning's military training school. As a war tax refuser, she has refused payment of all forms of federal income tax since 1980.

"I believed that if the general public, especially the American public, had access to the information [I released] this could spark a domestic debate on the role of the military and our foreign policy in general as it related to Iraq and Afghanistan. I also believed the detailed analysis of the data over a long period of time by different sectors of society might cause society to reevaluate the need or even the desire to even engage in counterterrorism and counterinsurgency operations that ignore the complex dynamics of the people living in the effected environment everyday."

—Chelsea Manning

CPSIA information can be obtained at www.ICGtesting.com
Printed in the USA
BVOW04s0708010514

351674BV00010B/58/P

9 780983 083054